# winter
## recipe collection
### *by* Sainsbury's

100 delicious recipes for everyday inspiration

# Welcome...

...to the winter recipe collection by Sainsbury's. We've compiled some of our favourite recipes, and created some irresistible brand-new ones too, to give you everyday inspiration all winter long.

Each delicious recipe has been tried, tested and tasted by Sainsbury's, so you can be sure of great results, whatever your level of cooking expertise. All the dishes are made from readily available ingredients, with easy-to-follow, step-by-step instructions. The recipes are divided into clear sections, from soups and sides through to mains and desserts, so it's easy to find just what you need to feed your family. There's even a special Christmas section, full of inspiring festive ideas.

Prep and cooking times are provided, as well as nutritional information. The index at the back lists all recipes alphabetically and by main ingredient. And to help you quickly find the right dish at the right time, they're also listed under the following themes: no more than 5 ingredients, vegetarian, on the table in 45 minutes or less, special occasions and family favourites.

We hope you find plenty of inspiration to create fabulous meals, and that this cookbook becomes an indispensable addition to your kitchen. Happy cooking!

---

We've added these icons to make everything as clear as possible

 Recipes that can be on the table in 45 minutes or less

 Suitable for vegetarians

 Recipes containing 1 or more of your 5 a day, to help you plan for healthy eating

# contents

# soups

| | |
|---|---:|
| Pumpkin, sweet potato & red pepper soup | 8 |
| Broccoli & Stilton soup with crunchy Cheddar toasts | 10 |
| Carrot & cumin soup | 10 |
| Creamy mussel soup | 12 |
| Tomato & basil soup with garlic ciabatta bread | 14 |
| Leek & potato soup with crispy bacon & potato chunks | 16 |
| Mushroom & parsley soup | 16 |
| Moroccan red lentil & tomato soup | 18 |

Serves 4
Prep time: 20 minutes
Cook time: 55 minutes

# Pumpkin, sweet potato & red pepper soup

Full of nutritious, seasonal vegetables, this soup has a sweetish taste and the toasted seeds add an appetising crunch

3 x red peppers, halved and deseeded
1 tablespoon oil
1 red onion, peeled and finely chopped
1 clove garlic, peeled and crushed
1 tablespoon sun dried tomato purée
400g pumpkin flesh, chopped into chunks

400g sweet potato, peeled and chopped into chunks
1 litre vegetable stock
2 teaspoons pumpkin seeds
2 teaspoons sunflower seeds
2 teaspoons sesame seeds

1 Preheat the oven to 200°C, fan 180°C, gas 6.

2 Reserve one pepper half for the garnish, and roughly chop the remaining pepper halves. Set aside.

3 Heat the oil in a heavy-based pan and cook the onion and garlic for 10 minutes until soft. Stir in the sun dried tomato purée, pumpkin, sweet potato and peppers. Cook for 10 minutes, until beginning to colour.

4 Pour in the stock and bring to the boil. Cover with a lid and cook over a medium heat for 30 minutes, until the vegetables are soft.

5 Place all the seeds on a baking tray and toast in the oven for 5 minutes. Pour the soup into a food processor and blend until smooth.

6 Finely chop the reserved pepper half. Divide the soup between 4 bowls and garnish with a sprinkling of toasted seeds and chopped pepper.

Per serving: 218 cals, 5.3g fat, 0.8g sat fat, 17.2g total sugars, 0.1g salt

Did you know...?
All Sainsbury's pumpkins are British

'Toasted seeds add an inviting crunch to this vibrant vegetable soup'

Serves 4
Prep time: 15 minutes
Cook time: 30 minutes

# Broccoli & Stilton soup

## with crunchy Cheddar toasts

This rich and creamy soup is a great way to use up leftover Stilton

| | |
|---|---|
| 1 tablespoon olive oil | 350g broccoli, cut into florets |
| 25g unsalted butter | 4 slices cut from a crusty white baton |
| 1 leek (approx 100g), finely chopped | 60g Cheddar, sliced |
| 400g Maris Piper potatoes, peeled and cubed | 50g Stilton |
| 1.3 litres vegetable stock | 80ml double cream |

1   Heat the oil in a large saucepan over a medium heat then add the butter, leek and potatoes and cook for 10 minutes. Pour in the stock and bring to the boil. Add the broccoli, then cover and simmer for 15 minutes.

2   Meanwhile, toast the baton slices under a preheated grill until golden on both sides. Top with the Cheddar and grill until browned and bubbling.

3   Crumble the Stilton into the soup, then blend in a food processor until smooth. Stir in the cream, season with freshly ground black pepper and serve topped with the cheese toasts.

Per serving: 462 cals, 29g fat, 18.6g sat fat, 3.3g total sugars, 0.8g salt

## Carrot & cumin soup

Heat 1 tablespoon olive oil and 25g butter in a large pan. Add 1 peeled and chopped onion and cook, stirring, for 5 minutes. Add 500g chopped carrots and 2 teaspoons ground cumin and cook for 2 minutes. Add 100ml dry white wine and cook to reduce by half. Add 500ml veg stock, bring to the boil, then simmer for 25 minutes. Cool, then blend in batches until smooth. Return to the pan, season and reheat gently. Serve garnished with chopped chives.

**SERVES 4**   Prep time: 15 minutes   Cook time: 50 minutes

Serves 4
Prep time: 20 minutes
Cook time: 30 minutes

# Creamy mussel soup

This elegant recipe is ideal for a dinner party

1kg fresh mussels (from Sainsbury's fish counter)
200ml white wine
1 tablespoon olive oil
1 large onion, peeled and chopped
1 red chilli, deseeded and finely chopped

2 cloves garlic, peeled and crushed
750ml fish stock ($\frac{1}{2}$ x fish stock cube)
200ml single cream
juice of $\frac{1}{2}$ a lemon
Sainsbury's pea shoots, to garnish

1 De-beard the mussels and discard any broken or open ones.

2 Bring the wine to the boil in a large pan. Tip in the mussels, cover and cook for 5 minutes until the mussels are opened (discard any that don't open). Drain, reserving the leftover juices. Set aside 4 mussels and shell the rest.

3 Return the pan to the heat and add the oil. Cook the onion, chilli and garlic, stirring for 10 minutes until soft. Pour the reserved mussel juices through a sieve into the onion mixture and add the stock. Bring to a simmer and cook for a further 10 minutes.

4 Whizz the soup in a blender until smooth, then return to the pan and add the mussels and cream. Gently heat for a further 5 minutes (do not boil).

5 At the last minute, stir in the lemon juice, spoon into bowls and garnish with a few pea shoots. Add one mussel in its shell to each bowl for decoration.

Per serving: 125 cals, 5.9g fat, 6.4g sat fat, 5.9g total sugars, 0.5g salt

Did you know...?
Mussels are at their best in cold weather, so they are usually in season from October to March

**Serves 4**
Prep time: 20 minutes
Cook time: 40 minutes

# Tomato & basil soup
## with garlic ciabatta bread

Nutritious and homely, this herby tomato soup is sure to become a favourite, especially when served with the easy garlic bread

1 tablespoon olive oil, plus extra for drizzling
1 onion, peeled and finely chopped
1 celery stick, finely chopped
1 tablespoon tomato purée
1kg tomatoes, quartered, hard cores removed
1 litre vegetable stock
½ x 28g pack Sainsbury's fresh basil, chopped
3 sprigs fresh rosemary, finely chopped

**FOR THE GARLIC BREAD**
4 cloves garlic, peeled and roughly chopped
2 tablespoons fresh parsley, finely chopped
75g unsalted butter, softened
1 ciabatta

1 Heat the oil in a large, heavy-based pan over a low heat. Add the onion and celery and cook for 10 minutes, until soft and lightly browned.

2 Add the tomato purée and mix well. Add the tomatoes and a generous grinding of black pepper and stir well. Cover with a lid and cook for 10 minutes over a low heat.

3 Pour in the stock, stir well and bring to the boil. Turn the heat down to low and replace the lid. Cook gently for 20 minutes, stirring occasionally.

4 Meanwhile, preheat the oven to 200°C, fan 180°C, gas 6. Stir the garlic and parsley into the butter. Using a bread knife, make incisions in the ciabatta 2cm apart, but don't slice right through. Use a knife to spread garlic butter between the slices. Wrap the ciabatta in foil and bake for 10 minutes, then remove the foil and bake for a further 6–8 minutes to make the crust crispy.

5 Stir the basil through the soup, then remove from the heat and leave to stand for a few minutes to cool slightly. Pour into a food processor and blend until the tomatoes are broken down. Serve topped with rosemary, a drizzle of olive oil and freshly ground black pepper.

**Per serving: 424 cals, 26g fat, 12.2g sat fat, 12.2g total sugars, 0.9g salt**

Serves 4
Prep time: 15 minutes
Cook time: 35 minutes

# Leek & potato soup

## with crispy bacon & potato chunks

Crispy bacon gives this warm and comforting soup an exciting twist

| | |
|---|---|
| 1 tablespoon olive oil, plus extra to drizzle | 20g unsalted butter |
| 1 onion, peeled and roughly chopped | 1 litre vegetable stock |
| 2 leeks, roughly chopped | 6 slices streaky bacon |
| 600g potatoes, peeled and chopped | 1 tablespoon parsley, roughly chopped |

1 Heat the oil in a large saucepan and tip in the onion, leeks, potatoes and butter. Cook for 5-10 minutes.

2 Add the stock and bring to the boil. Cover and simmer for 20 minutes, until the potato is soft. Meanwhile, grill the bacon until crispy, then chop into strips.

3 Once the soup is ready, remove some of the potato chunks, cool slightly and chop into small cubes. Set aside.

4 Blend the soup in a food processor until almost smooth, then divide between 4 bowls. Top with the potato chunks, bacon strips and parsley. Season with freshly ground black pepper and serve drizzled with olive oil.

**Per serving: 370 cals, 21.4g fat, 5.6g sat fat, 5g total sugars, 1.1g salt**

## Mushroom & parsley soup

In a large pan, fry 2 peeled, chopped onions in 2 tablespoons olive oil for 5 minutes. Add 500g chopped chestnut mushrooms and 250g peeled, chopped potatoes, fry for 2 minutes, then add 600ml veg stock and 300ml milk. Simmer for 15 minutes, add ½ x 28g pack Sainsbury's fresh flat-leaf parsley and blend in a food processor. Season and serve.

**SERVES 4**   Prep time: 10 minutes   Cook time: 25 minutes

Serves 4
Prep time: 15 minutes
Cook time: 40 minutes

# Moroccan red lentil & tomato soup

Make this flavoursome veggie soup as spicy as you like by adding extra chilli

1 large onion, peeled and finely chopped
2 sticks celery, finely chopped
1 red pepper, deseeded and chopped
2 cloves garlic, peeled and crushed
2 tablespoons olive oil
1 teaspoon ground coriander
1 teaspoon smoked paprika
1 teaspoon ground chilli
1 stick cinnamon
1 tablespoon tomato purée

2 teaspoons caster sugar
2 x 390g cartons Sainsbury's premium chopped tomatoes
200g dried red lentils
1 litre vegetable stock
1 x 410g tin chick peas, drained and rinsed
juice of 1 lemon
1 x 25g pack Sainsbury's fresh coriander, chopped

1  In a food processor, blend the onion, celery, red pepper and garlic to a purée. Heat the oil in a large pan and cook the purée for around 5 minutes.

2  Stir in the coriander, smoked paprika and chilli. Add the cinnamon stick and cook for about 1 minute, until fragrant. Add the tomato purée, sugar, tomatoes, lentils and vegetable stock. Bring to the boil, then cover and simmer for a further 30 minutes.

3  Tip in the chick peas and cook for a further 5 minutes, topping up with water if necessary. Season to taste. Stir through the lemon juice and chopped coriander just before serving.

Per serving: 273 cals, 8.6g fat, 0g sat fat, 15.5g total sugars, trace salt

Try... serving your soup with pitta bread and any of Sainsbury's delicious varieties of houmous for a filling vegetarian meal

# winter salads

| | |
|---|---|
| Chick pea salad with pitta croutons | 22 |
| Butternut squash & mozzarella salad | 24 |
| Chorizo, red pepper, butter bean & spinach salad | 26 |
| Hot potato salad with mackerel, rocket & avocado | 28 |
| Smoky potato salad | 28 |
| Warm lentil & avocado salad | 30 |
| Chicory, walnut & Roquefort salad | 32 |
| Ginger & quinoa chicken salad | 32 |
| Veggie sausage, butternut squash & red pepper salad | 34 |
| Moroccan-style aubergine salad | 36 |
| Warm mushroom & bacon salad | 38 |
| Pear, walnut & Dolcelatte salad | 38 |

**Serves 4**
Prep time: 10 minutes
Cook time: 20 minutes

# Chick pea salad with pitta croutons

The pitta croutons add a moreish crunch to this salad, and the feta-style cheese provides zing. For an extra kick, toss in a finely chopped red chilli

6 white pitta breads, torn into pieces
2 tablespoons olive oil
1 medium cucumber, peeled, deseeded and thickly sliced
4 spring onions, finely chopped
3 tomatoes, deseeded and each sliced into 8 pieces
2 x 410g tins Sainsbury's chick peas, drained

1 x 200g pack be good to yourself Greek salad cheese, crumbled
1 x 28g pack Sainsbury's fresh mint, leaves removed and torn
juice of 2 lemons
2 tablespoons extra-virgin olive oil
150g young leaf spinach
a handful of fresh flat-leaf parsley leaves

1 Preheat the oven to 180°C, fan 160°C, gas 4.

2 Place the pittas in a roasting dish, toss with the olive oil and season with salt and freshly ground black pepper. Cook for 15–20 minutes, until crispy but not completely hard. Meanwhile, sprinkle ½ teaspoon salt over the cucumber and set aside for 10 minutes.

3 In a bowl, mix together the spring onions, tomatoes, chick peas, cheese and mint leaves. Whisk the lemon juice with the extra-virgin olive oil, season and drizzle over the chick pea mixture. Add the cucumber.

4 Arrange the spinach in a large serving bowl, then add half the pitta croutons and spoon over the chick pea mixture. Sprinkle with the remaining pitta croutons and the parsley, then serve.

Per serving: 578 cals, 21.3g fat, 10g sat fat, 6.4g total sugars, 1.8g salt

Did you know...?
You'll find all sorts of healthier cheeses in Sainsbury's be good to yourself range, including farmhouse cheese, mozzarella and garlic & parsley roulé

‘This colourful salad gives you a taste of the Med’

**Serves 4**
Prep time: 10 minutes
Cook time: 40 minutes

# Butternut squash & mozzarella salad

The buttery, sweetish flavour of the squash is enhanced by roasting and it combines beautifully with mozzarella and sunflower seeds

1 butternut squash

2 tablespoons olive oil, plus extra for drizzling

8 cloves garlic, peeled

2 tablespoons sunflower seeds

1 x 70g pack Sainsbury's wild rocket

1 x 125g pack basics mozzarella pearls, torn

1 Preheat the oven to 190°C, fan 170°C, gas 5.

2 Slice and deseed the butternut squash and place in a roasting tin. Toss with the oil, garlic and sunflower seeds. Season with salt and freshly ground black pepper, then roast for 35–40 minutes until tender, turning halfway through cooking. Allow to cool slightly.

3 Combine the squash with the rocket leaves, mozzarella and the juices left in the roasting tin. Drizzle with olive oil and serve for a tempting salad or side dish.

**Per serving: 278 cals, 17.6g fat, 8g sat fat, 9.3g total sugars, 0.4g salt**

Did you know...?
The seeds of a butternut squash are tasty when toasted

**Serves 4**
Prep time: 15 minutes
Cook time: 5 minutes

# Chorizo, red pepper, butter bean & spinach salad

The sweet flavours of the roasted red peppers temper the spiciness of the chorizo in this hearty salad

½ x 390g Revilla chorizo, skin removed, sliced
1 x 410g tin Sainsbury's butter beans, drained and rinsed
½ x 450g jar Karyatis roasted red peppers, drained and chopped

1 x 100g pack Sainsbury's young leaf spinach
1½ tablespoons sherry vinegar

1 Dry fry the chorizo in a large non-stick frying pan until crispy. Transfer to a plate lined with kitchen paper and set aside.

2 Add the beans and peppers to the same pan and heat through for 1-2 minutes in the residual oil from cooking the chorizo.

3 Place the spinach in a large bowl and pour over the beans and any juices from the pan. Serve drizzled with sherry vinegar and sprinkled with the chorizo.

**Per serving: 367 cals, 23.2g fat, 8.2g sat fat, 3.2g total sugars, 1.4g salt**

**Love your leftovers**
Cut leftover chorizo into bite-sized pieces and fry. Serve as a quick and tasty party food idea with cocktail sticks and mustard for dipping

**Serves 4**
Prep time: 10 minutes
Cook time: 15 minutes

# Hot potato salad
## with mackerel, rocket & avocado

The zesty, mustardy dressing helps cut through the richness of the mackerel

550g Taste the Difference Vivaldi salad potatoes
1 tablespoon wholegrain mustard
1 tablespoon white wine vinegar
1½ tablespoons olive oil
juice of ½ a lemon

½ x red onion, peeled and thinly sliced
½ x 70g pack Sainsbury's wild rocket leaves
1 avocado, peeled, stoned and cut into chunks
1 x 250g pack Sainsbury's hot smoked mackerel fillets

1  Place the potatoes in a large saucepan and cover with water. Bring to the boil and simmer for about 15 minutes, until the potatoes are tender. Drain. When the potatoes are cool enough to handle, cut them in half. Place in a large bowl.

2  In a small bowl, whisk the mustard, vinegar, oil and lemon juice together. Pour the dressing over the potatoes and toss to coat well.

3  Add the red onion, rocket and avocado, and flake in the smoked mackerel. Gently mix together and serve.

Per serving: 453 cals, 31.5g fat, 11g sat fat, 2.3g total sugars, 1.9g salt

## Smoky potato salad

Boil 750g Taste the Difference Anya potatoes, halved, until tender. Drain. Mix together 3 teaspoons crushed mustard seeds, ½ teaspoon smoked paprika, 60ml mayonnaise and the zest and juice of 1 lemon. Place the potatoes in a serving bowl with 3 sliced hard-boiled eggs. Stir in the dressing. Season and sprinkle over chopped fresh dill. Great with steamed fish.

**SERVES 4**  Prep time: 10 minutes   Cook time: 18 minutes

*Full of vitality, this salad is packed with nutrients and flavour*

Serves 4
Prep time: 10 minutes
Cook time: 27 minutes

# Warm lentil & avocado salad

A variety of textures add interest to this warm salad. Be good to yourself Greek salad cheese has a lusciously creamy feel with fewer calories than normal feta

2 red onions, peeled and cut into eighths
1 tablespoon balsamic vinegar
250g cherry tomatoes
2 ripe avocados, peeled, stoned and cut into bite-sized pieces
50g wild rocket

1 tablespoon extra-virgin olive oil
2 x 410g tins Sainsbury's green lentils, drained and rinsed
200g be good to yourself Greek salad cheese, crumbled

1 Preheat the oven to 200°C, fan 180°C, gas 6.

2 Place the onions in a roasting tin and pour over the vinegar and 1 tablespoon water. Season and roast for 15 minutes, stirring halfway through.

3 Add the tomatoes and cook for a further 10-12 minutes until they burst.

4 Place the avocado in a large bowl. Add the rocket, drizzle over the oil and season.

5 Remove the tomatoes and onions from the oven. Add the lentils, stirring well - the heat of the tin will warm them through. Add the lentil mixture to the salad and stir. Sprinkle over the cheese and serve.

Per serving: 376 cals, 21.8g fat, 7.7g sat fat, 8.8g total sugars, 0.9g salt

### Did you know...?
Tinned lentils are a healthy storecupboard standby. Low in fat and high in protein, they also have a low GI rating, which means you feel fuller for longer

*This warm salad is full of exciting tastes and textures*

**Serves 6**
Prep time: 10 minutes
Cook time: 4 minutes

# Chicory, walnut & Roquefort salad

This impressive, chef-style salad has sharp, tangy flavours

1 x 100g pack Sainsbury's walnut halves
1 x 180g pack (2 heads) Sainsbury's chicory
2 x 75g packs Sainsbury's watercress leaves
2 x 150g packs Taste the Difference Roquefort

**FOR THE DRESSING**
2 tablespoons cider vinegar
2 teaspoons runny honey
2 tablespoons olive oil

1 Heat a small frying pan over a medium heat and toast the walnut halves for 3–4 minutes. Leave to cool slightly.

2 Pull away two-thirds of the outer leaves of each chicory head and arrange them between 6 plates. Thinly slice the remaining chicory vertically and place on top of the chicory leaves with a handful of watercress on each. Crumble on the Roquefort and the toasted walnuts.

3 Place the cider vinegar, honey and olive oil in a bowl, season with freshly ground black pepper and mix well. Drizzle over the salad and serve.

**Per serving:** 353 cals, 30.5g fat, 13.7g sat fat, 6.4g total sugars, 0.2g salt

## Ginger & quinoa chicken salad

Cook 300g quinoa following pack instructions, adding 1 teaspoon turmeric to the water. Fry 3 chicken breasts, cut into 3cm cubes, in 1 tablespoon olive oil until cooked. Add 150g chopped dried apricots and 50g chopped walnuts and set aside. Mix together 2 tablespoons white wine vinegar, 1 tablespoon olive oil, 1 teaspoon caster sugar and 3cm ginger, peeled and grated. Mix the chicken into the quinoa, stir in 8 thinly sliced spring onions and the dressing, and serve.

**SERVES 4**  Prep time: 15 minutes  Cook time: 25 minutes

**Serves 4**
Prep time: 15 minutes
Cook time: 35 minutes

# Veggie sausage, butternut squash & red pepper salad

You don't have to be vegetarian to enjoy this substantial salad - the flavours work equally well with meaty sausages

2 tablespoons olive oil
8 Cauldron Lincolnshire vegetarian sausages
1 small butternut squash (about 400g), peeled, deseeded and diced
2 red peppers, deseeded and cut into strips
4 leeks, washed, trimmed and cut into 2cm pieces

½ x 15g pack Sainsbury's fresh thyme, stalks removed
½ teaspoon smoked paprika
200g quinoa
750ml Sainsbury's Signature vegetable stock

1  Heat 1 tablespoon oil in a large frying pan and cook the sausages for 5-6 minutes. Transfer to a board, cut into 2cm chunks and set aside.

2  Heat the remaining 1 tablespoon oil, add the butternut squash and cook for 10 minutes, stirring occasionally until browned.

3  Add the peppers and leeks. Cook for 2-3 minutes, stirring to coat well, then add the sausages along with the thyme, paprika, quinoa and stock.

4  Cover and cook for 15 minutes until everything is tender, then serve.

Per serving: 443 cals, 14.6g fat, 2g sat fat, 16.9g total sugars, 1.3g salt

### Wine match
With the sweetness from the red peppers and the butternut squash, this dish needs to be matched with a bold, fruity red like a peppery Shiraz

**Serves 4**
Prep time: 15 minutes
Cook time: 20 minutes

# Moroccan-style aubergine salad

Pepped up with Moroccan spice and red chilli, this tempting salad will perk up your taste buds

2 medium aubergines, sliced lengthways into pieces about 1cm thick
3 tablespoons olive oil
200g white bread, torn into small, bite-sized pieces
1 teaspoon Moroccan spice mix

½ x large red chilli, deseeded and finely chopped
½ x 200g pack Sainsbury's SO organic Greek feta, crumbled
½ x 28g pack Sainsbury's fresh mint, leaves only, stalks discarded and large leaves torn

1 Preheat the oven to 200°C, fan 180°C, gas 6.

2 Heat a griddle pan until hot and brush the aubergine slices with 2 tablespoons oil. Cook in batches over a low heat for about 5 minutes on each side, or until chargrilled and just tender. Set aside.

3 Meanwhile, toss the bread pieces with the spice mix. Spread out on a baking tray and cook in the oven for about 10 minutes, until crunchy and golden.

4 Arrange the aubergine slices on a plate, scatter with the chilli, crunchy croutons, feta and mint. Season with salt and freshly ground black pepper and serve drizzled with the remaining 1 tablespoon oil.

Per serving: 365 cals, 22.6g fat, 11.2g sat fat, 5.4g total sugars, 1.6g salt

**Love your leftovers**
Whizz any leftover white bread in a blender, then freeze the breadcrumbs and use to coat fishcakes or as a topping for pasta bakes or casseroles

'This spicy Moroccan-inspired salad packs quite a punch'

**Serves 4**
Prep time: 5 minutes
Cook time: 12 minutes

# Warm mushroom & bacon salad

Garlic mushrooms work well with the robust flavours of bacon and blue cheese

25g unsalted butter
1 clove garlic, peeled and finely sliced
1 x 250g pack Sainsbury's chestnut mushrooms, quartered
3 tablespoons olive oil
1 small ciabatta, torn into bite-sized pieces

½ x 300g pack Sainsbury's 10 unsmoked back bacon, chopped
2 fresh rosemary sprigs, leaves only
1 tablespoon red wine vinegar
1 x 70g pack Sainsbury's wild rocket
100g basics blue cheese, crumbled

1 Melt half the butter in a frying pan over a medium-high heat. Add the garlic and mushrooms and cook for 5 minutes, until golden. Set aside in a bowl.

2 In the same pan, melt the remaining butter with 1 tablespoon olive oil. Add the ciabatta, bacon and rosemary. Cook for 5 minutes or until crispy, then set aside on kitchen paper.

3 Toss the mushrooms with the vinegar and remaining 2 tablespoons oil, and season with salt and freshly ground black pepper.

4 Divide the rocket between 4 plates and scatter over the bacon mixture. Spoon over the mushrooms and dressing, scatter with cheese, then serve.

**Per serving: 488 cals, 32.4g fat, 13.9g sat fat, 1.7g total sugars, 2.6g salt**

## Pear, walnut & Dolcelatte salad

Preheat the oven to 200°C, fan 180°C, gas 6. Bake 50g walnut pieces in a roasting tray for 10 minutes. Core and thinly slice 3 pears, then mix with 100g rocket, 150g chopped Dolcelatte and the nuts. Whisk 100ml extra-virgin olive oil with 50ml maple syrup, 50ml cider vinegar and 1 tablespoon wholegrain mustard. Season. Drizzle over the salad to serve.

**SERVES 4** Prep time: 10 minutes   Cook time: 10 minutes

# savoury pies & bakes

# Steak & ale pies

**Serves 4**
Prep time: 25 minutes,
plus 1 hour marinating
Cook time: 2 hours,
45 minutes

The crisp filo topping on these pies adds an interesting variation
to the classic steak and ale combo

1½ x 454g packs Sainsbury's lean diced
casserole steak
1 x 500ml bottle Taste the Difference
traditional Kentish ale
2 cloves garlic, peeled and crushed
1 teaspoon juniper berries
2 stalks fresh rosemary, leaves of 1 chopped
2 tablespoons cornflour
3 tablespoons olive oil

1 large onion, peeled and sliced
1 x 250g pack Sainsbury's closed cup
mushrooms, quartered
2 carrots, peeled and cut into rounds
300ml beef stock (½ x stock cube)
1 tablespoon redcurrant jelly
4 sheets Sainsbury's fresh filo pastry
1 egg, beaten
rocket leaves, to serve

1 Place the steak in a bowl. Add the ale, garlic, juniper berries and the whole
  stalk of rosemary, and marinate for at least 1 hour.

2 Drain the steak, reserving the ale and discarding the other bits. Toss the
  meat with the cornflour.

3 Heat 2 tablespoons oil in a large pan. Brown the meat in batches until golden
  brown all over. Remove from the pan with a slotted spoon and set aside.

4 Add 100ml of the ale to the pan along with the onion. Stir, scraping off any
  bits stuck to the bottom of the pan. Cook for 10 minutes, until the onion is
  softened. Add the mushrooms and carrots and cook for another 2 minutes.

5 Return the meat to the pan, along with any juices, and add the remaining
  ale, stock and the chopped rosemary. Bring to the boil, then cover with a
  lid and simmer for 2 hours over a low heat. At the end of cooking, stir in
  the redcurrant jelly, then divide the mixture between 4 small pie dishes.

6 Preheat the oven to 200°C, fan 180°C, gas 6. Brush the sheets of filo
  lightly with the remaining 1 tablespoon oil. Crumple them up and use to
  top each pie, then brush with the egg. Bake in the oven for 15 minutes.
  Serve with rocket leaves.

**Per serving: 430 cals, 17g fat, 4.6g sat fat, 8.3g total sugars, 0.6g salt**

**Serves 4**
Prep time: 45 minutes,
plus 15 minutes' chilling
Cook time: 1½ hours

# Creamy chicken & tarragon pie

Chicken and tarragon work beautifully together in this wonderfully creamy pie filling. For a richer topping, try using Sainsbury's all-butter puff pastry

500g Sainsbury's British skinless and boneless chicken thigh fillets
1 tablespoon vegetable oil
300g shallots, peeled and halved
1 large courgette, sliced
2 leeks, washed and cut into 2.5cm chunks
2 tablespoons plain flour, plus extra to dust
1 x 500ml pouch Sainsbury's Signature chicken stock

½ x 20g pack Sainsbury's fresh tarragon, chopped
150g petits pois, frozen or fresh
150ml British half-fat crème fraîche
200g shortcrust pastry
1 medium egg, lightly beaten

1 Cut each thigh into 3 pieces. Heat the oil in a large frying pan and fry the chicken pieces for 5-10 minutes, until golden brown. Remove from the pan and set aside.

2 In the same frying pan, fry the shallots, courgette and leeks over a high heat for 3-4 minutes, until they begin to colour.

3 Add the flour, stirring, and cook for 1 minute. Gradually pour in the stock, stirring, until it's all used up. Return the chicken to the pan along with the tarragon. Bring to the boil, then simmer for 30 minutes.

4 Remove from the heat and add the petits pois and crème fraîche. Spoon into a 1.5-litre lipped baking dish.

5 Preheat the oven to 220°C, fan 200°C, gas 7. Roll out the pastry on a floured surface to the thickness of a £1 coin. Cut the pastry into narrow strips that measure the length of the dish. Twist and weave together to create a lattice pattern over the top of the pie, keeping some aside for the edge. Trim off any excess, then lay the strips around the lip of the dish. Press down and crimp with a fork. Brush the pastry with the egg to glaze.

6 Chill for 15 minutes to set the pastry, then bake for 30-35 minutes until golden.

**Per serving: 713 cals, 40.7g fat, 18.1g sat fat, 8.9g total sugars, 0.9g salt**

**Serves 4**
Prep time: 20 minutes
Cook time: 35 minutes

# Mushroom & turkey pot pies

These individual pies taste as good as they look, and the mushroom soup filling makes them really easy to make

1 x 375g pack Sainsbury's ready-rolled puff pastry, at room temperature
1 tablespoon olive oil
1 onion, peeled and finely chopped
1 clove garlic, peeled and crushed

200g chestnut mushrooms, sliced
1½ tablespoons chopped fresh rosemary
600g mushroom soup
400g cooked turkey, cut into small chunks
1 tablespoon milk, for glazing

1 Preheat the oven to 200°C, fan 180°C, gas 6. Unroll the pastry and cut out 4 circles a little larger than the top of a 300ml pie dish. Place on a baking tray and chill in the fridge for at least 30 minutes.

2 Meanwhile, heat the oil in a large saucepan over a medium heat and gently fry the onion and garlic for 3-4 minutes until softened. Add the mushrooms and rosemary and cook for a further 5 minutes until softened.

3 Pour in the mushroom soup, then stir in the turkey. Season with freshly ground black pepper. Divide the mixture between 4 x 300ml pie dishes. Wet the rim of each pie dish with water, cover each with a circle of pastry and press the pastry over the sides to seal. Brush the pie tops with milk and bake in the oven for 20-25 minutes, until risen and golden.

Per serving: 649 cals, 36.2g fat, 12.7g sat fat, 5.8g total sugars, 1.8g salt

### Did you know...?
Sainsbury's only sells 100% British turkeys. Our Taste the Difference turkeys are also free range, Freedom Food and, from this Christmas, from Woodland Farms

**Serves 6**
Prep time: 45 minutes
Cook time: 3 hours,
15 minutes

# Comforting beef bourguignon pie

The slow cooking of the meat enhances the sumptuous flavours of this pie

2 tablespoons olive oil
600g braising steak, cut into large cubes
1 medium white onion, peeled and sliced
3 cloves garlic, peeled and roughly chopped
25g plain flour
500ml red wine
400ml beef stock (1 stock cube)
½ x 20g pack Sainsbury's fresh rosemary

1 bay leaf
½ x 250g pack Sainsbury's smoked bacon lardons
½ x 250g pack Sainsbury's chestnut mushrooms, halved
2 red onions, peeled and cut into wedges
350g shortcrust pastry
1 egg, beaten

1  Heat half the oil in a large saucepan or flameproof casserole dish. Fry the beef in batches until browned all over, then remove from the pan and set aside.

2  Reduce the heat to low, then cook the white onion and garlic in the remaining 1 tablespoon oil for 5 minutes until soft. Return the meat to the pan and stir in the flour. Cook for a further 2 minutes, stirring all the time. Gradually stir in the wine, then add the stock, rosemary and bay leaf, stirring constantly until boiling. Cover and simmer for 1 hour.

3  In a different pan, fry the bacon, mushrooms and red onions together for 2-3 minutes, then transfer to the beef pan. Cover and simmer for another hour, then remove the lid and cook for 30 minutes, until the gravy has thickened.

4  Preheat the oven to 200°C, fan 180°C, gas 6. Roll out the pastry to about ¾cm thick. Cut out a pastry lid a little larger than the top of a 2-litre pie dish. Keep the leftover pastry for the rim.

5  Moisten the rim of the pie dish with a little water, then press a pastry strip around it. Fill the dish with the beef mixture. Moisten the pastry rim with a little water, top with the pastry lids and pinch the pastry together all the way around to seal. Cut two small slits in the top of the pie so steam can escape.

6  Brush all over with egg and bake for 30 minutes, or until golden and bubbling.

Per serving: 580 cals, 33.6g fat, 14.9g sat fat, 6.2g total sugars, 1.9g salt

> Red wine gives beef an irresistible flavour

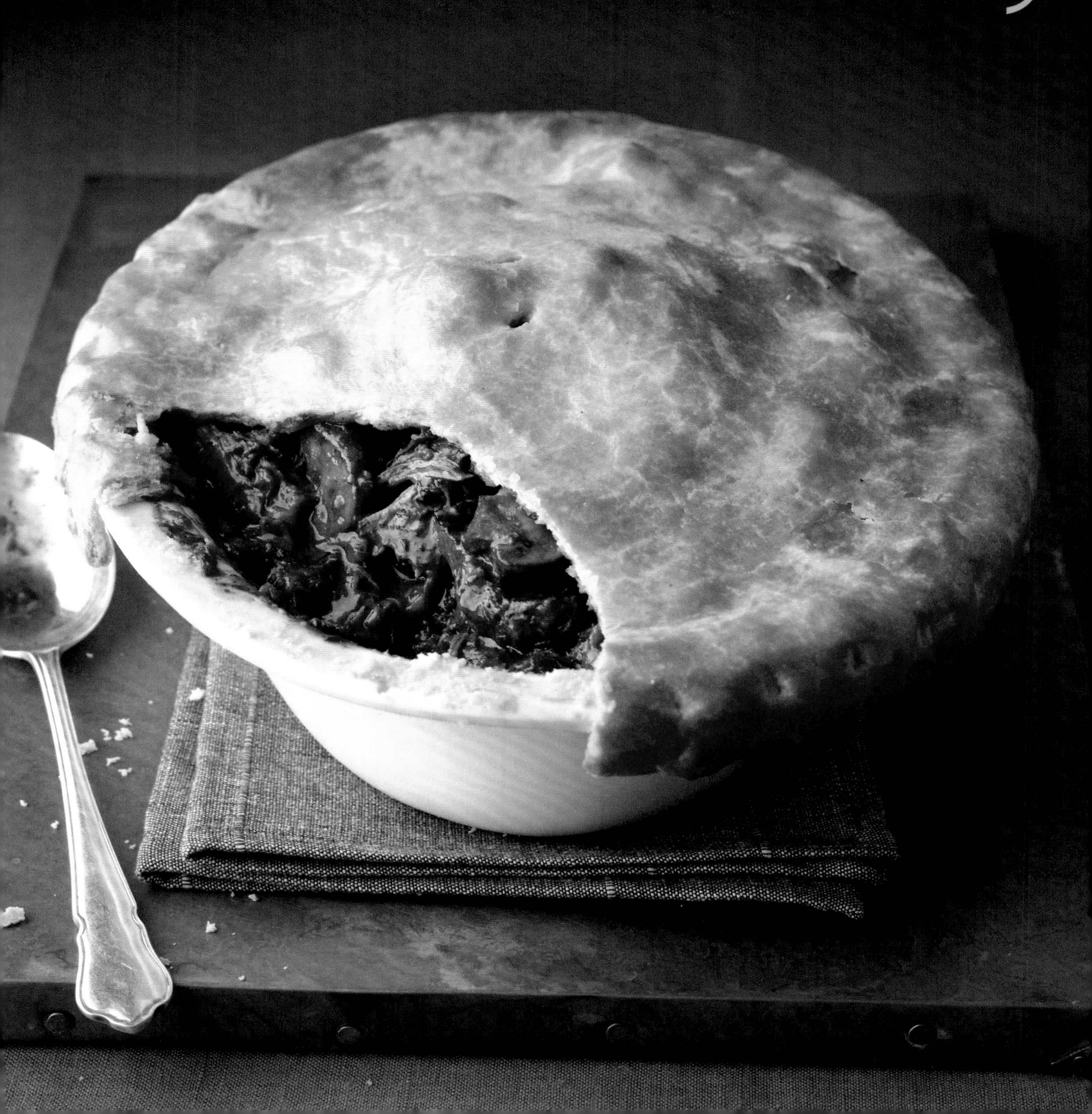

**Serves 4**
Prep time: 25 minutes
Cook time: 1½ hours

# Roast chicken, squash & leek filo pie

Using roast chicken gives this pie a fabulously full flavour, and the soft cheese lends a lovely creamy, herby note to the filling

400g butternut squash, peeled, deseeded and cut into 4cm cubes
2 teaspoons olive oil
1 cooked rotisserie chicken
1 large leek, washed and thinly sliced
1 teaspoon cornflour

75g Sainsbury's light soft cheese with garlic & herbs
100ml chicken stock (½ x stock cube)
50g breaded ham slices, torn
40g unsalted butter, melted
½ x 270g pack Jus Rol filo pastry sheets

1 Preheat the oven to 200°C, fan 180°C, gas 6. Place the squash in a roasting tin, drizzle over half the olive oil and season. Roast for 30 minutes, turning halfway through cooking.

2 Meanwhile, carefully take the chicken off the carcass, then discard the skin and bones. Shred the meat with a fork.

3 Heat the remaining 1 teaspoon olive oil in a pan on the hob and cook the leek, covered, over a low heat for 12 minutes. Add the cornflour, cheese and stock, then cook, stirring, for a couple of minutes. Add the roasted squash, chicken and ham, then remove from the heat and leave to cool.

4 To assemble the pie, lightly brush some of the butter on the insides of a 23cm pie dish, and brush over one sheet of the filo pastry. Lay the buttered pastry sheet across the base of the dish, then layer the rest of the sheets, overlapping the sides to go all the way round the dish like the spokes of a wheel.

5 Spoon the chicken mixture into the centre of the pie dish and fold the overlapping filo in over the top of the pie. Brush generously with melted butter. Bake for 40-45 minutes.

Per serving: 461 cals, 22g fat, 9.6g sat fat, 6.7g total sugars, 1.6g salt

An exciting new twist on a chicken and ham pie

**Serves 4**
Prep time: 20 minutes
Cook time: 55 minutes

# Luxury three-fish pie with spinach

Capers add a deliciously piquant contrast to the fish and potato in this easy pie

750g Desirée potatoes, peeled and chopped
4 spring onions, trimmed and sliced
1 x 200g bag Sainsbury's young leaf spinach
350g skinless, boneless, salmon fillet, cut
into 2cm pieces
125g raw king prawns, defrosted if frozen

225g skinless smoked haddock fillet, cut
into 2cm pieces
2 tablespoons capers, chopped
500ml half-fat crème fraîche
1 1/2 tablespoons cornflour, dissolved in
a little water

1 Preheat the oven to 200°C, fan 180°C, gas 6. Boil the potatoes for 15 minutes until cooked, then drain and mash. Stir in the spring onions and season.

2 Cook the spinach following pack instructions, then squeeze out any excess water. Spread the salmon, prawns and haddock evenly in the bottom of a 20 x 20cm ovenproof dish, then spread the spinach over the fish.

3 Place the capers and crème fraîche in a pan and gently bring to simmering point. Stir in the cornflour and heat until the crème fraîche has thickened. Season, and pour over the fish. Top with the mash and bake for 40 minutes.

Per serving: 579 cals, 22.4g fat, 11.3g sat fat, 5.4g total sugars, 1.6g salt

## Individual salmon fillet pie

Preheat the oven to 200°C, fan 180°C, gas 6. Lay 4 x 260g Sainsbury's Scottish skinless salmon fillets (the flatter and wider, the better) in an ovenproof dish and spread over 150g light soft cheese mixed with 15g finely chopped fresh chives. Spoon 1 x 400g pack Sainsbury's mashed potato on top, then brush with melted butter. Bake for 12–14 minutes, until the fish is cooked through and the potato is crispy on top.

**SERVES 4**  Prep time: 8 minutes  Cook time: 12–14 minutes

**Serves 6**
Prep time: 35 minutes
Cook time: 1 hour

# Lamb moussaka

## with tomatoes & peppers

Roasting the peppers and aubergines deepens the flavour of the vegetables, making this a tasty classic that never fails to impress

2 aubergines (approx 500g), sliced into rounds
2 red peppers, deseeded and quartered
1 tablespoon olive oil
1 onion, peeled and finely chopped
1 clove garlic, peeled and crushed
1/2 teaspoon ground cinnamon
pinch ground allspice
1 x 500g pack Sainsbury's lamb mince

200ml white wine
1 x 390g carton Sainsbury's chopped tomatoes in tomato juice
zest of 1 lemon
50g unsalted butter
50g plain flour
500ml semi-skimmed milk
2 egg yolks
30g parmesan, grated

1  Preheat the oven to 190°C, fan 170°C, gas 5. Place the aubergine slices and peppers on separate baking trays, brush with a little of the oil and roast in the oven for 30 minutes.

2  Meanwhile, heat the remaining oil in a large saucepan and fry the onion and garlic for 5 minutes until soft. Stir through the cinnamon and allspice, then add the lamb. Stir well, increase the heat and cook for 4–5 minutes until the lamb is browned. Add the wine, tomatoes and lemon zest. Bring to the boil, then reduce to a simmer and cook for 20 minutes, until thick.

3  In a separate pan, melt the butter over a low heat, stir in the flour and cook for 2 minutes. Gradually add the milk, stirring continuously, until the mixture becomes a thick sauce. Simmer for 4 minutes, stirring regularly, then remove from the heat and stir in the egg yolks.

4  Line the bottom of a 2-litre ovenproof dish with half the aubergines. Cover with half the lamb mixture and 2/3 of the white sauce. Layer with the remaining aubergine, peppers and lamb mixture, and drizzle with the remaining white sauce. Sprinkle with grated parmesan and bake in the oven for 30 minutes. Leave to stand for 5 minutes before serving.

**Per serving: 481 cals, 30.8g fat, 13.8g sat fat, 11.6g total sugars, 0.6g salt**

**Serves 6**
Prep time: 20 minutes
Cook time: 50 minutes

# Spanakopita lasagne

This is a delicious vegetarian cross between the popular Greek pastry and spinach dish spanakopita ('spinach pie') and a classic Italian lasagne

---

1 x 200g pack Sainsbury's young leaf spinach
3 large free-range eggs
½ x 200g pack Sainsbury's SO organic Greek feta cheese
½ onion, peeled and roughly chopped
1 x 28g pack Sainsbury's flat-leaf parsley

1 x 700g jar Sainsbury's Italian passata sauce
1 x 250g pack Sainsbury's fresh egg lasagne sheets
1 x 125g pack be good to yourself mozzarella, grated

---

1 Preheat the oven to 180°C, fan 160°C, gas 4. Place the spinach in a microwaveable bowl with 2 tablespoons water. Microwave on high for 3 minutes, then drain and squeeze out the excess water.

2 Crack the eggs into a mixing bowl, crumble in the feta and whisk well. Set aside. Whizz the spinach, onion and parsley in a food processor until finely chopped, then stir into the egg mixture.

3 Pour a layer of passata sauce into the bottom of a 2-litre baking dish. Cover with 1 layer of lasagne and spread with a quarter of the spinach mixture. Repeat these layers 3 times, then add a final layer of pasta, top with passata sauce and sprinkle with mozzarella. Bake for 50 minutes until golden.

Per serving: 243 cals, 11.7g fat, 2.8g sat fat, 6.7g total sugars, 1g salt

**Serves 6**
Prep time: 10 minutes
Cook time: 20 minutes

# Bacon & mushroom pasta bake

This hearty, full-flavoured bake is sure to become a family favourite

1 x 500g pack Sainsbury's wholewheat
fusilli pasta
1 tablespoon olive oil
1 red onion, peeled and chopped
2 cloves garlic, peeled and chopped
100g streaky bacon, cut into small pieces
150g chestnut mushrooms, quartered

2 tablespoons green pesto
2 x 400g cartons basics chopped tomatoes
a handful of fresh flat-leaf parsley, leaves
only, roughly chopped
100g Sainsbury's grated mozzarella
25g freshly grated parmesan

**1** Preheat the oven to 200°C, fan 180°C, gas 6.

**2** Cook the pasta following pack instructions. Meanwhile, heat the oil in a medium pan and add the onion, garlic, bacon and mushrooms. Cook for about 5 minutes, until the onion is soft and the bacon is golden. Add the pesto, tomatoes and parsley. Season with freshly ground black pepper. Bring to the boil, then remove from the heat.

**3** Drain the pasta and mix with the sauce. Pour into a 2-litre baking dish. Top with the mozzarella and parmesan and bake for 10 minutes, until the cheese has melted.

Per serving: 461 cals, 15.8g fat, 6.2g sat fat, 9.1g total sugars, 1.2g salt

**Love your leftovers**
Fry leftover bacon until crispy, and crumble into
a soup for a delicious twist on croutons

**Serves 4**
Prep time: 15 minutes
Cook time: 25 minutes

# Squash & rosemary pasta bake

The herby cheese topping makes this vegetable bake extra satisfying

750g butternut squash, peeled, deseeded
and chopped into 2cm cubes
2 large onions, peeled and sliced
2 tablespoons olive oil
40g fresh white breadcrumbs
15g freshly grated parmesan

2 small fresh rosemary stalks, leaves only,
finely chopped
300g Sainsbury's whole and white penne
250ml vegetable stock ($\frac{1}{2}$ x stock cube)
a good grating of whole nutmeg
green salad, to serve

1 Preheat the oven to 220°C, fan 200°C, gas 7.

2 Place the squash and onion on 2 separate baking trays. Season and toss
each with 1 tablespoon oil. Roast for 20 minutes, turning halfway through.
Meanwhile, mix together the breadcrumbs, parmesan and rosemary to
make the topping, and cook the pasta following pack instructions.

3 Place half the roasted veg in a food processor, along with the stock and
nutmeg. Season with salt and freshly ground black pepper and blend
until smooth.

4 Drain the pasta and toss through the squash sauce. Stir in the remaining
roasted veg, then tip into a 1.5-litre ovenproof dish and sprinkle on the
breadcrumb mixture.

5 Place under a grill preheated to high, and grill until lightly golden. Serve
with a green salad.

**Per serving:** 471 cals, 8.7g fat, 2g sat fat, 18g total sugars, 0.8g salt

**Serves 4**
Prep time: 25 minutes
Cook time: 45 minutes

# Sausage & red pepper savoury bread pudding

If the family love sweet bread pudding, why not try this savoury version?

1 tablespoon olive oil
1 onion, peeled and thinly sliced
2 Karyatis roasted red peppers, chopped
6 Sainsbury's Butcher's Choice half-fat pork sausages, cooked and cut into 2cm slices
400g stale white bread, crusts removed, cut into 3cm cubes

15g fresh basil leaves, torn
100g mature Cheddar, grated
5 medium eggs
200ml semi-skimmed milk

1 Preheat the oven to 200°C, fan 180°C, gas 6.

2 Heat the oil in a large frying pan over a medium heat. Add the onion and cook until soft and just beginning to brown. Stir in the red peppers and cooked sausages, then allow to cool.

3 In a 1.5- or 2-litre ovenproof dish, toss the bread cubes with the basil, half the cheese and the cooled sausage mixture.

4 In a small bowl, whisk the eggs and milk together and season with freshly ground black pepper. Pour the egg mixture over the rest of the ingredients in the ovenproof dish, stirring gently to combine.

5 Sprinkle the remaining grated cheese on top and bake for 35-40 minutes, until puffed up and golden brown.

Per serving: 740 cals, 34.8g fat, 13.6g sat fat, 8.8g total sugars, 2.9g salt

Did you know...?
All Sainsbury's fresh sausages are 100% British

# roasts

roasts

**Serves 4**
Prep time: 5 minutes
Cook time: 1 hour,
20 minutes

# Juicy apricot chicken

This simple glaze will give your roast chicken a fruity boost

1 Taste the Difference free-range whole chicken (approx 1.5kg)
60g apricot jam

2 tablespoons wholegrain mustard
10g fresh thyme, separated into sprigs

1  Preheat the oven to 190°C, fan 170°C, gas 5. Place the chicken in a roasting tin and cook for 1 hour, 20 minutes (20 minutes per 500g, plus 20 minutes).

2  Place the jam, mustard and small sprigs of thyme in a small saucepan, and gently melt over a low heat.

3  Brush the apricot glaze over your chicken 20 minutes before the end of cooking. Great served with roast potatoes and a selection of vegetables.

**Per serving: 227 cals, 8.3g fat, 2.2g sat fat, 9.1g total sugars, 0.5g salt**

**Wine match**
Chardonnay is the perfect match for roast chicken, and a lightly oaked example would be great with this dish

‘ A sweet, spicy glaze
adds zing to a simple
roast chicken ’

**Serves 2**
Prep time: 5 minutes
Cook time: 15 minutes
plus 5 minutes to rest

# Pecan-crusted duck

This nutty topping pairs exceptionally well with the flavour of duck

50g pecans
25g unsalted butter
½ x 28g pack Sainsbury's fresh flat-leaf parsley

¼ teaspoon ground cinnamon
2 x Taste the Difference Gressingham duck breast fillets, skin removed

1 Preheat the oven to 200°C, fan 180°C, gas 6. Place the pecans, butter, parsley and cinnamon in a blender and whizz until it's a chunky paste.

2 Spread the mixture over the tops of the duck breasts and pat gently. Place on a baking tray and bake for 15 minutes, then remove from the oven and allow to rest for 5 minutes. Slice in half diagonally and serve. Great with roast potatoes and a selection of vegetables.

Per serving: 439 cals, 36g fat, 10.7g sat fat, 1.2g total sugars, 0.4g salt

### Wine match
The rich flavours of the duck and its nutty topping are best matched with an intensely fruity red wine, such as a Chilean Merlot

# Roast lamb & lentil casserole

Lamb shoulder is a succulent, flavoursome cut that's perfect with lentils and vegetables in this delicious casserole

**Serves 6**
Prep time: 15 minutes
Cook time: 2 hours,
plus 5 minutes to rest

1.5kg whole, easy-carve lamb shoulder
1 tablespoon olive oil
1 medium onion, peeled and finely sliced
1 large clove garlic, peeled and finely sliced
4 carrots, diced
1 small swede, peeled and diced

3 potatoes, peeled and diced
600ml lamb stock (1 stock cube)
1 x 410g tin green lentils, drained
2 tablespoons capers
1 x 28g pack Sainsbury's fresh flat-leaf parsley, chopped

1 Preheat the oven to 220°C, fan 200°C, gas 7. Place the lamb in a large, ovenproof casserole dish and roast for 25 minutes.

2 Meanwhile, heat the oil in a frying pan and cook the onion and garlic for 3-4 minutes until soft. Add the carrots and swede, and cook for 10 minutes, until golden.

3 Remove the lamb from the oven and reduce the temperature to 200°C, fan 180°C, gas 6. Add the veg and potatoes around the lamb, then pour over the stock. Cover and cook in the oven for 1 hour, 25 minutes.

4 Remove the casserole from the oven, stir in the lentils and return to the oven for 10 minutes.

5 Remove the lamb shoulder from the casserole dish, leave to rest for 5 minutes, then shred the meat off the bone. Stir back into the veg and serve garnished with capers and parsley.

Per serving: 598 cals, 33.5g fat, 14g sat fat, 10.9g total sugars, 0.1g salt

**Serves 8**
Prep time: 25 minutes
Cook time: 3 hours,
15 minutes

# Beef brisket pot roast

Slow cooking makes the beef pot roast joint in this hearty recipe deliciously tender and appetising

1 tablespoon olive oil
1 beef pot roast joint (approx 1.5kg)
250ml red wine
1 red onion, peeled and chopped
1 bunch of celery, roughly chopped
2 cloves garlic, peeled and crushed
1 bay leaf
½ x 1kg pack Sainsbury's carrots, chopped

½ x 15g pack Sainsbury's fresh thyme, separated into sprigs
2 x 500ml pouches Sainsbury's Signature beef stock
1 x 390g carton Sainsbury's chopped tomatoes
1 heaped teaspoon Sainsbury's harissa paste

1 Preheat the oven to 160°C, fan 140°C, gas 3.

2 Heat the olive oil in a large, ovenproof casserole pot. Add the beef and brown on all sides. Add all the remaining ingredients and bring to the boil.

3 Cover with a lid, then cook in the oven for 3 hours or until the meat is tender. Season to taste, then slice the meat and serve with the vegetables and sauce. Great with mashed potato.

Per serving: 479 cals, 32.1g fat, 12.9g sat fat, 7.3g total sugars, 0.4g salt

# Cider roast pork

## with mincemeat stuffing

Apples are a great match for pork, so adding cider takes this a natural step further. The tangy mincemeat stuffing adds a surprising twist

**Serves 8**
Prep time: 15 minutes
Cook time: 2 hours,
20 minutes, plus
10 minutes to rest

1.35kg boneless pork shoulder joint
25g unsalted butter
1 tablespoon runny honey
1 red and 1 green apple, cored and quartered
100ml dry cider
a few sage leaves, to garnish

**FOR THE STUFFING**
1 tablespoon olive oil
1 medium onion, peeled and finely chopped
100g ready-to-eat chestnuts, chopped
60g ready-to-eat apricots, chopped
150g fresh breadcrumbs
5 tablespoons mincemeat
1 medium egg, beaten
3 tablespoons fresh flat-leaf parsley, chopped

1 Preheat the oven to 190°C, fan 170°C, gas 5. Remove and reserve the string from the pork, open it out and season well.

2 To make the stuffing, heat the oil in a large pan. Fry the onion for 5 minutes, then mix with the remaining stuffing ingredients, reserving 25g chestnuts for the garnish. Season well.

3 Reserving enough stuffing to make some balls, spread the rest over the inside of the pork, re-roll up and secure with string. Place the pork in a large roasting tin and cook in the oven for 1 hour (cover with foil if it starts to burn).

4 Melt the butter and mix with the honey and apples. Place the stuffing balls and apples around the pork and pour the cider around the joint (not over the skin). Roast for a further 1 hour, 15 minutes, then rest for 10 minutes. Untie and slice the pork. Garnish with the sage and the remaining chestnuts. Great with a selection of vegetables.

Per serving: 575 cals, 33.1g fat, 11.3g sat fat, 15.8g total sugars, 0.7g salt

# Veggie mushroom nut roast

**Serves 8**
Prep time: 15 minutes
Cook time: 50 minutes,
plus 10 minutes to rest

Vegetarians and meat eaters alike will love this mushroom nut roast, full of flavoursome ingredients

2 tablespoons olive oil, plus extra for oiling tin
1 large onion, peeled and chopped
2 cloves garlic, peeled and chopped
250g mushrooms, chopped
3 x 100g packs Sainsbury's walnut halves
100g wholemeal breadcrumbs
50g sunflower seeds, toasted

50g pumpkin seeds, toasted
1 teaspoon fresh thyme leaves, plus extra sprigs to garnish
1 Sainsbury's Woodland free-range egg, beaten
1 tablespoon soy sauce
100g Sainsbury's extra-mature British Cheddar

1   Oil a 1.5-litre loaf tin and line the base with a strip of baking parchment. Preheat the oven to 180°C, fan 160°C, gas 4.

2   Heat the olive oil in a frying pan and add the onion, garlic and mushrooms. Slowly cook until golden brown.

3   Blend the walnuts in a food processor until finely ground. In a bowl, combine the mushroom mixture with the walnuts, breadcrumbs, seeds, thyme leaves, egg, soy sauce and most of the cheese. Season with freshly ground black pepper.

4   Pile the mixture into the loaf tin, smooth the top and sprinkle on the rest of the cheese. Bake for 30-40 minutes, or until the mixture feels firm. Allow to rest in the tin for 10 minutes, then turn out and garnish with the sprigs of thyme. To serve, slice with a sharp knife. Great with green beans and sweet potato mash.

**Per serving: 493 cals, 41.2g fat, 6.4g sat fat, 3.4g total sugars, 0.8g salt**

# side dishes

Serves 8
Prep time: 10 minutes
Cook time: 1 hour,
5 minutes

# Parsnip, potato & spinach gratin

This deliciously creamy vegetable gratin is great served with roast chicken or lamb chops

1 tablespoon olive oil
1 onion, peeled and finely chopped
800g parsnips, peeled and cut into angular shapes
450g potatoes, peeled and cut into ½ cm slices

1 x 300ml pot Sainsbury's double cream
500ml Sainsbury's 1% fat milk
a little freshly grated nutmeg
100g baby spinach leaves

1  Preheat the oven to 180°C, fan 160°C, gas 4.

2  Heat the oil in a heavy-based pan, then lightly fry the onion. Add the parsnips, potatoes, cream and milk. Season with salt, freshly ground black pepper and the nutmeg, then stir. Simmer for 20 minutes or until the vegetables are tender.

3  Stir through the spinach, pour into an ovenproof dish and bake for 45 minutes.

**Per serving: 326 cals, 21.2g fat, 11.6g sat fat, 11.1g total sugars, trace salt**

Did you know...?
Parsnips are at their best after a spell of cold weather, as the frost intensifies their sweet flavour

Serves 8
Prep time: 20 minutes
Cook time: 25 minutes

# Cheesy cabbage & potato wraps

This fun way to serve potatoes and cabbage will get the kids interested in veg!

1 medium Savoy cabbage
500g Maris Piper potatoes, peeled and cut into chunks

1 leek, washed and thinly sliced
100g basics full-flavour Cheddar, grated

1   Preheat the oven to 200°C, fan 180°C, gas 6. Blanch 8 large cabbage leaves for 3 minutes, then place in a bowl of cold water. When cool, drain and set aside.

2   Core the remaining cabbage and finely shred. Boil the potatoes for about 10 minutes, until tender. Add the shredded cabbage and leek for the last 5 minutes of the cooking time. Drain well, return to the pan and mash together. Stir in 80g cheese and season with freshly ground black pepper.

3   Lay out the blanched cabbage leaves and divide the potato mixture between them. Gather each cabbage leaf together to create a package, with some of the potato mixture still exposed. Sprinkle with the remaining cheese.

4 Cook in the oven for 10-15 minutes, until the cheese is bubbling.

**Per serving: 124 cals, 4.8g fat, 3.2g sat fat, 3.3g total sugars, 0.3g salt**

## Creamy root vegetable mash

Peel and chop 500g potatoes, 500g carrots and 500g parsnips, and place in a large pan of boiling water. Boil for about 15-20 minutes, until tender, then drain well. Return the veg to the same pan and mash to a coarse purée. Mix in 1 tablespoon butter and 2 tablespoons crème fraîche, and season to taste with salt and freshly ground black pepper. Great with the sausage & mash with caramelised red onion sauce on page 96 instead of traditional mash.

SERVES 6 Prep time: 10 minutes   Cook time: 15-20 minutes

Serves 4
Prep time: 10 minutes
Cook time: 45 minutes

# Garlicky carrots

Roasting whole bulbs of garlic gives a more mellow, almost sweet flavour. Serve this attractive selection of veg in the tray and let everyone help themselves

700g carrots, peeled and sliced in
half lengthways
1 x pack basics garlic

2 oranges, zest and juice
1 tablespoon olive oil

1 Preheat the oven to 200°C, fan 180°C, gas 6. Place the carrots in a large roasting tin with the whole garlic bulbs. Mix in the orange zest and juice and place the squeezed halves in the tray.

2 Drizzle with olive oil and season with salt and freshly ground black pepper. Bake for 45 minutes, turning the carrots halfway through.

**Per serving: 97 cals, 3.7g fat, 1g sat fat, 11.3g total sugars, 0.2g salt**

## Steamed broccoli with toasted sesame seeds

Trim 600g broccoli into florets and steam until tender. Toss with 1 teaspoon sesame oil and serve sprinkled with 1 tablespoon toasted sesame seeds for a side dish with a lovely oriental flavour.

**SERVES 4** Prep time: 5 minutes   Cook time: 8 minutes

'Roasting carrots with orange halves really brings out their sweetness'

Serves 4
Prep time: 10 minutes
Cook time: 45 minutes

# Mozzarella & bacon stuffed aubergine

These roasted, stuffed aubergines are oozing with irresistible flavours – they make a great starter for a special meal

---

2 medium-sized aubergines
1 x 125g pack be good to yourself mozzarella, sliced

80g onion, peeled and thinly sliced
125g streaky bacon, sliced

---

1 Preheat the oven to 180°C, fan 160°C, gas 4. Gently slice slits into the aubergines, about 1.5cm apart, taking care not to cut through to the bottom.

2 Place in a baking dish and stuff the slits alternately with slices of mozzarella, onion and bacon. Bake for 45 minutes, until the aubergine is soft and the bacon is crisp.

**Per serving: 152 cals, 10g fat, 4.3g sat fat, 4.3g total sugars, 1g salt**

## Stir-fried chilli Savoy cabbage

Heat 1 tablespoon olive oil in a deep frying pan. Add 8 peeled, sliced shallots and stir-fry over a high heat for 3 minutes. Add 2 peeled, sliced cloves garlic and 1 deseeded, sliced red chilli. Cook, stirring, for 2 minutes, then remove from the pan. Add ½ tablespoon oil and 100ml water to the pan and stir-fry 1 medium Savoy cabbage, chopped and stalks removed, for 3-4 minutes, until cooked but still crunchy. Stir in the shallot mixture and season, then serve.

**SERVES 6** Prep time: 10 minutes   Cook time: 8-9 minutes

Serves 10
Prep time: 15 minutes
Cook time: 20 minutes

# Cumin & coriander potato fritters

These spiced-up fritters go well with roast lamb, or you can enjoy them as a starter with soured cream

500g Taste the Difference Vivaldi potatoes, peeled, grated and excess water squeezed out
10g fresh coriander leaves, finely chopped
1 teaspoon ground cumin

½ x red chilli, deseeded and finely chopped
4 tablespoons plain flour
1 egg, beaten
2 tablespoons olive oil

1 Preheat the oven to 180°C, fan 160°C, gas 4. Combine all the ingredients, except the oil, in a bowl and form into small patties using about 3 tablespoons of the mixture for each one. Set aside in the fridge to firm up or until you're ready to cook.

2 Heat a little olive oil in a large frying pan over a medium-high heat. Fry the fritters on both sides, in batches, using up the remaining oil as needed, until they begin to brown. Place on a baking tray.

3 Bake the fritters in the oven for 10 minutes to ensure the potatoes are cooked through.

**Per serving: 96 cals, 3g fat, 0.7g sat fat, 0.5g total sugars, trace salt**

## Spicy sweet potato wedges

Preheat the oven to 220°C, fan 200°C, gas 7. Cut 3-4 sweet potatoes into chunky wedges and place on a baking tray. Drizzle over 1 tablespoon olive oil and toss well. Sprinkle with ½ teaspoon sea salt and some dried chilli flakes (½ teaspoon will give a bit of a kick, 1 teaspoon will give a more fiery flavour). Cook for 25-30 minutes, until the sweet potato is soft. Sprinkle over ½ teaspoon sea salt and serve with a small bowl of mayonnaise for dipping.

SERVES 4 Prep time: 5 minutes   Cook time: 25-30 minutes

Serves 4
Prep time: 10 minutes
Cook time: 30 minutes

# Braised celery

## with bacon & courgettes

The punchy flavours in this dish make it a tasty starter

| | |
|---|---|
| 1 head of celery, trimmed and roughly chopped | 1 medium onion, peeled and finely chopped |
| 750ml vegetable stock | 2 large courgettes (about 300g), finely diced |
| 1 tablespoon olive oil | ½ x 25g pack Sainsbury's fresh thyme, separated into sprigs |
| 125g smoked back bacon, cut into small strips | 4 tablespoons single cream |

1 Place the celery in a shallow pan. Add the stock, bring to the boil and simmer for 15-20 minutes until tender. Remove with a slotted spoon and set aside, reserving 150ml of the liquid.

2 Meanwhile, heat the oil in a frying pan. Cook the bacon and onion for 5-7 minutes, until the onion is soft and the bacon golden. Add the courgettes, thyme and celery.

3 Cook for 1-2 minutes, then pour over the reserved stock. Cook for a further 3-4 minutes, until the courgettes are tender. Stir in the cream, season and serve.

**Per serving: 174 cals, 11.2g fat, 4.3g sat fat, 4.8g total sugars, 0.8g salt**

# winter warmers

Serves 4
Prep time: 20 minutes
Cook time: 20 minutes

# Sweet potato chilli

Sweet potato gives a creamy texture and slight sweetness to this hearty, nutritious vegetarian chilli

1 tablespoon olive oil
1 medium onion, peeled and roughly chopped
2 cloves garlic, peeled and crushed
1 red chilli, deseeded and finely chopped
1 teaspoon ground cumin
1 teaspoon chilli powder
1 red pepper, deseeded and diced
450g sweet potato, peeled and diced into 1cm cubes
1 teaspoon caster sugar

2 x 390g cartons Sainsbury's chopped tomatoes
1 x 410g tin Sainsbury's black-eyed beans, drained and rinsed
1 x 410g tin Sainsbury's red kidney beans, drained and rinsed
chopped fresh coriander, to serve
natural yogurt, to serve
toasted pitta bread, to serve

1  Heat the oil in a large casserole pot over a medium-high heat. Sauté the onion, garlic and chilli for 2 minutes. Add the spices, red pepper and sweet potato and cook for another 2 minutes.

2  Stir in the sugar, tomatoes, beans and 200ml water. Cover and simmer for about 15 minutes, until the sweet potato is tender. Season with salt and freshly ground black pepper to taste.

3  Just before serving, stir in the coriander. Serve with natural yogurt and warm pitta bread.

**Per serving: 555 cals, 5.9g fat, 1g sat fat, 23.5g total sugars, 1g salt**

Did you know...?
Sweet potatoes, as their name suggests, have a slightly sweet flavour. They are a source of vitamin C and can be cooked in similar ways to ordinary potatoes

This spicy vegetarian chilli is quick and easy to cook

Serves 4
Prep time: 10 minutes
Cook time: 30 minutes

# Sausage & mash
## with caramelised red onion sauce

The sweetness of the chutney and red wine gives these pork sausages a wonderful flavour, and as a sauce it makes for a great alternative to gravy

1 tablespoon olive oil
8 pork sausages
1 x 350g jar Taste the Difference caramelised red onion chutney
150ml red wine

150ml chicken stock
fresh thyme leaves from 2 small sprigs
2 x 400g packs Sainsbury's mashed potato, to serve
1 cabbage, chopped and steamed, to serve

1  Heat the oil in a large frying pan and cook the sausages for 5 minutes, shaking the pan often, until they are well browned.

2  Add the red onion chutney, wine, stock and thyme, and stir well until combined. Bring to the boil and simmer gently, uncovered, for 20 minutes, until the sauce has reduced and thickened. Be careful, as the sauce will be very hot. If the chutney becomes 'jam-like' during cooking, use a little extra hot stock to thin it down again.

3  Serve with the mash, heated through, and steamed cabbage.

Per serving: 627 cals, 26.3g fat, 12.4g sat fat, 32.6g total sugars, 3g salt

### Did you know...?
Outdoor-reared sausages from Sainsbury's instore meat counters are made with only prime cuts of shoulder and belly, with spices and fresh herbs. They're a bit bigger than other sausages for a really succulent texture, and are hand-linked in the traditional way

Serves 4
Prep time: 40 minutes
Cook time: 30 minutes

# Melanzane alla Parmigiana

Chargrilled aubergine, peppers and melted cheese are layered to make a mouthwatering classic Italian dish that's great for sharing

2 red peppers, halved lengthways and deseeded
2 medium aubergines, cut into 1cm thick slices
3 tablespoons olive oil
2 cloves garlic, peeled and finely chopped
1 x 340g jar Sainsbury's arrabbiata sauce

½ x 28g pack Sainsbury's fresh basil, roughly chopped
50g parmesan, finely grated
1 x 125g pack basics mozzarella cheese ball, torn into bite-sized chunks

1  Preheat the grill to medium-high. Grill the peppers cut-side down for about 15-20 minutes, until the skins are fully blackened. Carefully transfer to a bowl and cover tightly with clingfilm. Set aside for 10 minutes to allow the steam to loosen the skins.

2  Meanwhile, heat a griddle pan until hot and brush the aubergine slices with 2 tablespoons oil. Cook in batches over a low heat for about 5 minutes on each side, or until chargrilled and just tender. Set aside.

3  Preheat the oven to 180ºC, fan 160ºC, gas 4. Remove the peppers from the bowl, being careful to avoid the hot steam. Peel the skin from the peppers and discard.

4  In a separate pan, heat the remaining 1 tablespoon oil and gently fry the garlic for 2-3 minutes. Stir in the arrabbiata sauce, 150ml water and most of the basil. Bring to the boil, season well and remove from the heat.

5  Arrange a layer of peppers and aubergines in the bottom of a shallow 1.5-litre ovenproof dish. Pour over some of the sauce and sprinkle with a little parmesan. Repeat with the remaining ingredients, top with mozzarella and a final sprinkling of parmesan.

6  Bake for half an hour, until bubbling, then serve scattered with the remaining chopped basil.

**Per serving: 278 cals, 19g fat, 7g sat fat, 11.7g total sugars, 0.6g salt**

A classic Italian dish of peppers, aubergine and melting mozzarella

Serves 4
Prep time: 15 minutes
Cook time: 20 minutes

# Cranberry & Brie stuffed chicken

Delicious Brie and cranberry oozes from this impressive-looking dish

4 large (about 175g each) Sainsbury's skinless chicken breasts
80g Somerset Brie, sliced into thin strips
4 tablespoons Taste the Difference cranberry sauce
1 tablespoon chopped fresh thyme leaves

2 courgettes, peeled into ribbons
1 tablespoon olive oil
½ x 500g pack Sainsbury's cous cous
2 tablespoons chopped fresh flat-leaf parsley

1  Preheat the oven to 180°C, fan 160°C, gas 4. Cut a pocket in each of the chicken breasts horizontally, taking care not to slice the whole way through. Stuff the pockets with the sliced Brie, cranberry sauce and thyme.

2  Wrap the chicken breasts in the courgette ribbons until the filling is enclosed - use 6-8 ribbons to wrap each breast.

3  Place the chicken breasts on a baking tray, drizzle over the olive oil and season with salt and freshly ground black pepper. Cook in the oven for 20 minutes.

4  Meanwhile, make up the cous cous following pack instructions, then fork through the chopped parsley and season with salt and freshly ground black pepper.

5  Slice the chicken on the diagonal and serve with the cous cous.

Per serving: 622 cals, 12.1g fat, 3.3g sat fat, 11g total sugars, 0.3g salt

Did you know...?
The Maunder family began supplying Sainsbury's with chickens more than 100 years ago, and continue to do so today

Oozing Brie and a touch of cranberry make for an elegant dish

Serves 4
Prep time: 25 minutes
Cook time: 1 hour,
5 minutes

# Indian-spiced shepherd's pie

Indian spices and sweet potato give a special twist to a winter favourite

1.3kg sweet potato
1 tablespoon olive oil
1 x 500g pack Sainsbury's lamb mince
1 onion, peeled and chopped
2 cloves garlic, peeled and finely chopped
2 carrots, diced
1 teaspoon ground coriander
1 teaspoon ground cumin
1 teaspoon garam masala

¼ teaspoon hot chilli powder
1 tablespoon sun dried tomato purée
1 x 390g carton Sainsbury's chopped tomatoes
500ml lamb stock (½ x cube)
honey, to taste (optional)
25g unsalted butter
½ teaspoon cumin seeds
75g feta, crumbled

1 Preheat the oven to 180°C, fan 160°C, gas 4. Prick the sweet potatoes all over and bake in the oven for 30-40 minutes, or until soft. Meanwhile, heat half the oil in a large, heavy-based frying pan. Brown the mince, then remove from the pan and set aside. Drain off the lamb fat and discard.

2 Pour the remaining ½ tablespoon oil into the pan. Add the onion, garlic and carrots and fry gently for 10 minutes. Stir in the ground coriander, ground cumin, garam masala, chilli powder and tomato purée and cook for a further 2-3 minutes.

3 Return the mince to the pan and add the tomatoes and stock. Bring to the boil, then reduce the heat and simmer gently for 20 minutes. Season to taste with salt and freshly ground black pepper, and a little honey, if liked.

4 Meanwhile, melt the butter in a pan, add the cumin seeds and cook for 30 seconds or until fragrant. Scoop out the insides of the sweet potato into a bowl, discarding the skins, and add the butter-cumin mixture. Season well and mash together.

5 Spoon the mince into a 2-litre ovenproof baking dish and top with the mash. Sprinkle with crumbled feta and bake in the preheated oven for 25 minutes, until bubbling and golden.

Per serving: 842 cals, 38.9g fat, 20g sat fat, 25.9g total sugars, 1.7g salt

Serves 4
Prep time: 20 minutes
Cook time: 2 hours,
15 minutes

# Red-wine braised lamb shanks
## with thyme & rosemary

Wine and fresh herbs impart a wonderfully rich flavour to lamb cooked slowly for maximum tenderness - ideal for a special lunch

1 tablespoon olive oil
4 lamb shanks, bone in
2 red onions, peeled and halved
10 peppercorns
1 x 500ml pouch Sainsbury's Signature vegetable stock

½ x 20g pack Sainsbury's fresh rosemary, stalks removed
½ x 15g pack Sainsbury's fresh thyme, stalks removed, plus sprigs for garnishing
275ml red wine
1 tablespoon redcurrant jelly

1   Heat the oil in a large casserole pot on the hob. Add the lamb and brown on all sides. Add the onion, peppercorns, stock, herbs and wine. Bring to the boil, then cover and simmer for 2 hours.

2   Transfer the shanks to a dish, then bring the liquid in the pot to the boil and simmer for 10-15 minutes, until reduced by half. Stir in the redcurrant jelly. Return the shanks to the pot, then serve garnished with thyme. Great served with mash.

**Per serving: 481 cals, 26g fat, 9.1g sat fat, 3.6g total sugars, 3.8g salt**

## Creamy mushrooms on toast

Melt 25g unsalted butter with 2 peeled and finely chopped cloves garlic. Add 2 x 140g packs Taste the Difference exotic mushroom selection, tearing up any large ones, and fry for about 5 minutes until golden. Add 1 x 410g tin cannellini beans, drained, 75ml double cream and 1 x 15g pack fresh thyme, chopped, and simmer for 5 minutes to thicken. Serve on 4 slices of buttered toast.

**SERVES 4**  Prep time: 5 minutes  Cook time: 15 minutes

# Rustic Italian stew

Serves 4
Prep time: 20 minutes,
plus ½ hour marinating
Cook time: 1 hour,
10 minutes

Slow cooking with wine, herbs and garlic brings a wonderful flavour to this satisfying dish that makes a hearty lunch or supper

1 x 350g pack be good to yourself British diced lamb
1 onion, peeled and roughly chopped
2 carrots, chopped
2 cloves garlic, peeled and crushed
1 sprig rosemary
½ x red chilli, deseeded and chopped
1 shaving of orange zest
375ml red wine
1 tablespoon unsalted butter

1 tablespoon olive oil
1 tablespoon plain flour
1 x 390g carton Sainsbury's chopped tomatoes
250ml vegetable stock (1 stock cube)
1 teaspoon Taste the Difference balsamic vinegar
1 x 410g tin Sainsbury's butter beans or cannellini beans, drained

1 Place the lamb in a bowl with the onion, carrots, garlic, rosemary, chilli, orange zest and red wine. Leave to marinate in the fridge for 30 minutes (or longer if you have time).

2 Remove the meat with a slotted spoon, reserving the marinade, and fry it in the butter and oil until browned all over. Add the flour and stir for 1 minute. Stir in the marinade, tomatoes, stock and balsamic vinegar.

3 Cover and cook on the hob for about 1 hour, until the meat is tender. Add the beans, warm through and serve.

Per serving: 282 cals, 9.3g fat, 4.4g sat fat, 8.1g total sugars, 1g salt

Healthier living
With reduced fat for a healthier option, Sainsbury's be good to yourself British diced lamb is ideal for making an easy stew, such as the recipe above

A flavour-packed
and satisfying
rustic lamb stew

Serves 4
Prep time: 15 minutes
Cook time: 45 minutes

# Sausage & cider casserole

The flavours of cider and fresh apple work beautifully with pork sausages

1 tablespoon olive oil
8 Taste the Difference British pork & caramelised red onion sausages
1 x 1kg pack Taste the Difference Vivaldi salad potatoes
1 x 400g pack shallots, peeled and quartered
400g carrots, thickly sliced
25g plain flour

400ml dry cider
200ml chicken stock (½ x stock cube)
1 tablespoon fresh sage, chopped
1 tablespoon fresh thyme, chopped, plus extra to garnish
½ x 28g pack Sainsbury's fresh flat-leaf parsley, chopped
1 Braeburn apple, cored and diced

1  Preheat the oven to 200°C, fan 180°C, gas 6. Heat the oil in a large, ovenproof frying pan or flameproof casserole and gently fry the sausages until browned all over. Remove from the pan and set aside. Meanwhile, cook the potatoes in simmering water until just tender. Drain well and lightly crush with a fork. Set aside.

2  Drain off all but 1 tablespoon of the oil from the pan, add the shallots and carrots and cook over a medium heat for 5 minutes until golden. Reduce the heat, sprinkle in the flour and cook for 2 more minutes, stirring constantly.

3  Pour the cider and stock into the pan and bring to the boil, stirring all the time, until the sauce is smooth. Simmer for 5 minutes, until the sauce is thickened. Slice the sausages into pieces and add to the pan along with the fresh herbs. Season to taste with salt and freshly ground black pepper.

4  Combine the potatoes with the apple, season and spoon over the sausage casserole. Bake in the oven for 20 minutes, until golden and bubbling. To serve, scatter with a little fresh thyme.

Per serving: 662 cals, 25.3g fat, 7.1g sat fat, 23g total sugars, 2.2g salt

Try... making a vegetarian casserole. Use veggie stock and cooked vegetarian sausages instead

Sausages, cider and
sage combine perfectly
in this casserole

Serves 4
Prep time: 15 minutes
Cook time: 40 minutes

# Chicken & tomato stew

Packed with vegetables, this simple stew is perfect for a midweek supper

1 tablespoon olive oil
1 x 1.5kg whole chicken, cut into 8 pieces
1 x 250g pack Sainsbury's chestnut mushrooms, halved
1 red pepper, deseeded and cut into large chunks
1 yellow pepper, deseeded and cut into large chunks

½ x 400g pack Sainsbury's shallots, peeled
1 tablespoon tomato purée
100ml white wine
2 x 390g cartons Sainsbury's chopped tomatoes with garlic & olive oil
1 x 200g pack Sainsbury's young leaf spinach
2 tablespoons chopped fresh parsley

1 Warm the oil in a large, heavy-based pan over a medium-high heat and gently fry the chicken, skin-side down, until golden. Remove from the pan and set aside.

2 In the same pan, fry the mushrooms, peppers and shallots for 5 minutes over a medium-high heat. Stir in the tomato purée and pour in the wine. Heat for 1 minute, then stir in the chopped tomatoes and return the chicken to the pan.

3 Bring to the boil, then reduce the heat and simmer for another 30 minutes, stirring occasionally. Remove from the heat and stir in the spinach. Scatter over the parsley to serve. Great with mashed potato.

Per serving: 583 cals, 38.9g fat, 12.5g sat fat, 17.3g total sugars, 2.3g salt

Wine match
The predominant flavour here is tomato, so match this stew with a wine that has a zesty acidity, such as a Sauvignon Blanc

Serves 4
Prep time: 10 minutes
Cook time: 1 hour,
15 minutes

# Chunky beef casserole

A root vegetable and meat casserole with mushrooms for extra flavour

1 tablespoon olive oil
1 x 440g pack Sainsbury's beef braising steak, cut into chunks
1 tablespoon plain flour
½ x 400g pack Sainsbury's shallots, peeled
4 cloves garlic, peeled and chopped
1 x 500g pack Taste the Difference bunched carrots, topped
400g swede, peeled and cut into 4cm chunks

1 x 390g carton Sainsbury's chopped tomatoes
1 x 500g pouch Sainsbury's Signature beef stock
3 bay leaves
1 sprig of thyme, plus leaves from 1 extra sprig for garnishing
300g mushrooms, halved

1 Heat the oil in a large casserole dish. Toss the steak chunks in the flour and season well with salt and freshly ground black pepper. Fry the steak with the shallots and garlic for 5 minutes, until they begin to brown.

2 Stir in the carrots and swede and fry for 5 minutes, stirring occasionally. Pour in the tomatoes and stock, then add the bay leaves and the sprig of thyme. Bring to the boil, then cover with a lid and reduce the heat to a simmer.

3 Leave to simmer for 30 minutes, then stir in the mushrooms and cook for a further 30 minutes. Sprinkle with thyme and serve.

Per serving: 642 cals, 34.4g fat, 20.5g sat fat, 19.3g total sugars, 0.4g salt

Serves 4
Prep time: 15 minutes
Cook time: 1 hour

# Ratatouille & garlic bread cobbler

Slices of garlicky bread top this bean and Mediterranean vegetable casserole

3 tablespoons olive oil
1 large aubergine, cut into large chunks
2 red onions, peeled and cut into wedges
2 red peppers, deseeded and cut into large chunks
3 cloves garlic, peeled and roughly chopped
2 courgettes, cut into large chunks
250ml white wine

1 x 390g carton Sainsbury's chopped tomatoes
2 tablespoons sun dried tomato paste
2 x 400g tins Sainsbury's cannellini beans, drained and rinsed
1/2 x 28g pack Sainsbury's fresh flat-leaf parsley, chopped
1/2 x 310g pack Sainsbury's garlic baguette

1  Preheat the oven to 200°C, fan 180°C, gas 6. Heat half the oil in a large, ovenproof casserole dish, then add the aubergine and fry over a medium-high heat for 5 minutes until lightly charred. Remove from the pan and set aside.

2  Pour the remaining 1½ tablespoons oil into the pan. Add the onions and peppers and fry for 5 minutes, until softened and lightly charred. Reduce the heat and add the garlic and courgettes. Cook for 2–3 minutes then add the wine, tomatoes, tomato paste and 150ml water.

3  Add the aubergines and bring to the boil, then reduce the heat and simmer for 15 minutes. Stir in the cannellini beans and parsley, and season to taste with salt and freshly ground black pepper.

4  Cut the baguette into about 20 thin slices. Place them on top of the casserole, garlic-butter side up, and bake in the oven for 20 minutes until golden.

Per serving: 428 cals, 18.4g fat, 6.2g sat fat, 18.6g total sugars, 0.8g salt

Wine match
This richly flavoured vegetarian classic is great with either a red or white, so choose a southern French red like a Côtes du Rhône or opt for a Sauvignon Blanc

Serves 4
Prep time: 20 minutes
Cook time: 10 minutes

# Thai green curry mussel & prawn pot

Mussels and prawns cooked in a fragrant coconut Thai sauce make a dish that's great for sharing with friends

1 tablespoon olive oil
2 tablespoons Sainsbury's Thai green curry paste
1 x 400ml tin coconut milk
1 tablespoon fish sauce
1 stick of lemon grass, bruised
4 kaffir lime leaves (optional)

1kg mussels (from the fish counter), washed and beards removed (discard any that are open)
12 raw tiger prawns, shell and tail on
1 lime, quartered
2 green chillies, finely sliced

1  Heat the oil in a large pan and gently fry the curry paste for 1 minute, until it smells fragrant. Stir in the coconut milk, fish sauce, lemon grass and lime leaves, if using. Bring to the boil then throw in the mussels and prawns.

2  Cover the pan with a tight-fitting lid and leave to simmer for 5 minutes, occasionally shaking the pan, by which time the prawns should be cooked and the mussels should have opened - discard any mussels that are not open.

3  Squeeze the lime wedges over the curry and garnish with the sliced chilli to serve. Great served with French bread, to soak up the delicious sauce.

Per serving: 277 cals, 20.4g fat, 16.1g sat fat, 2.1g total sugars, 2.4g salt

Wine match
The complex flavours in this dish call for an aromatic white, and a zesty New Zealand Sauvignon Blanc is the perfect choice

*Fresh Thai flavours enhance the mussels and prawns in this dish*

Serves 6
Prep time: 15 minutes
Cook time: 40 minutes

# Cod, chorizo & chick pea stew

This easy-to-make, delicately spiced one-pot dish is packed with flavour and the chick peas add texture

2 tablespoons olive oil
2 onions, peeled and chopped
200g chorizo, sliced
1 red pepper, deseeded and sliced
1 yellow pepper, deseeded and sliced
2 cloves garlic, peeled and crushed
1 teaspoon sweet smoked paprika
½ x fish stock cube
pinch Sainsbury's saffron

2 x 390g cartons Sainsbury's chopped tomatoes
2 x 410g tins Sainsbury's chick peas, drained and rinsed
4 x 175g cod loin pieces, or other white fish, cut into large chunks
½ x 28g pack Sainsbury's fresh flat-leaf parsley, roughly chopped, to serve

1 Heat the oil in a large saucepan and cook the onions for 10 minutes. Add the chorizo and cook for a further 5 minutes. Add the peppers, garlic and paprika and continue to cook for 3–4 minutes.

2 Meanwhile, stir the stock cube and saffron into 200ml boiling water. Pour into the chorizo mixture and add the tomatoes and chick peas. Stir, season with salt and freshly ground black pepper, then cover and cook for 10 minutes.

3 Place the pieces of cod on top of the stew, then cover and cook for 8–10 minutes. Serve sprinkled with the parsley.

**Per serving: 284 cals, 14.9g fat, 4.1g sat fat, 8.6g total sugars, 1.3g salt**

Did you know...?
Sainsbury's was the first supermarket to sell MSC-certified sustainable cod

*Chorizo, chick peas and cod combine in this Spanish-inflenced dish*

Serves 4
Prep time: 15 minutes
Cook time: 45 minutes

# Sesame tuna & chips

This tasty, oriental twist on traditional fish and chips is healthier, too

1kg Maris Piper potatoes, unpeeled and cut into wedges
3 tablespoons olive oil

1 large red chilli, deseeded and finely sliced
2 tablespoons sesame seeds
4 x tuna steaks (approx 400g in total)

1 Preheat the oven to 220°C, fan 200°C, gas 7. In a large bowl, toss the potatoes with 2 tablespoons olive oil. Transfer to a baking dish and bake for 30 minutes. Add the chilli and cook for 15 minutes, occasionally shaking the pan, or until the potatoes are tender inside and crisp on the outside.

2 Meanwhile, sprinkle the sesame seeds over a plate. Dip one side of each of the tuna steaks into the seeds and set aside.

3 Heat the remaining 1 tablespoon oil in a large frying pan over a medium-high heat and fry the tuna steaks, sesame-seed side down to start, until cooked to your liking (3 minutes per side for medium-rare). Serve with the potato wedges and crushed minty peas (see recipe below).

Per serving: 445 cals, 16.8g fat, 3.7g sat fat, 1.6g total sugars, 0.2g salt

## Crushed minty peas

Place 240g Sainsbury's frozen petits pois and 10g fresh mint leaves in a saucepan and cover with 200ml cold water. Bring to the boil and simmer for about 5 minutes, until the peas are tender. Drain (reserving the water to adjust the consistency if necessary), then mash lightly with a potato masher. Season with salt and freshly ground black pepper. Set aside, keeping warm until ready to serve.

SERVES 4  Prep time: 5 minutes  Cook time: 7 minutes

Serves 4
Prep time: 15 minutes
Cook time: 30 minutes

# Pancetta-wrapped salmon

## with herby lentils

Baking salmon with pancetta and rosemary gives a delicious, intense flavour

225g puy lentils, rinsed
650ml vegetable stock (1 stock cube)
4 x salmon fillets (approx 150g each)
4 slices pancetta
4 small sprigs rosemary
1 tablespoon olive oil
1 red onion, peeled and finely sliced

2 tablespoons balsamic vinegar
250g baby plum tomatoes, halved
juice of ½ a lemon
1 x 28g pack Sainsbury's fresh flat-leaf parsley, finely chopped
100g young spinach

1  Preheat the oven to 200°C, fan 180°C, gas 6. Place the lentils in a pan and cover with the stock. Bring to the boil and simmer for 15-20 minutes, until tender. Drain off any excess stock, then set aside.

2  Wrap the salmon fillets in the sliced pancetta and transfer to a roasting tin lined with foil or baking parchment. Tuck the rosemary sprigs underneath the pancetta and bake in the oven for 10-12 minutes, until the salmon is cooked through.

3  Meanwhile, heat the olive oil in a large frying pan. Add the onion and cook for 5-6 minutes, until beginning to soften. Add the balsamic vinegar, tomatoes and cooked lentils and stir well. Stir through the lemon juice, parsley and spinach. Season to taste with salt and freshly ground black pepper, spoon onto 4 plates and serve topped with the salmon fillets.

**Per serving: 581 cals, 26.3g fat, 7.1g sat fat, 10.7g total sugars, 1.5g salt**

Serves 4
Prep time: 10 minutes
Cook time: 25 minutes

# Prawn & tomato curry

Fresh tomatoes and ginger add extra punch to this curry

5g unsalted butter
1 tablespoon olive oil
1 onion, peeled and chopped
1 x 2cm piece ginger, peeled and grated
1 tablespoon mild curry powder
1 x 390g carton Sainsbury's chopped tomatoes
250ml vegetable stock (½ x stock cube)

1 x 250g pack Taste the Difference pomodorino tomatoes, halved
¼ teaspoon sugar
1 x 250g pack basics cooked & peeled prawns
cooked basmati rice, to serve
half-fat crème fraîche or yogurt, to serve
10g fresh coriander, chopped, to serve

1 Melt the butter with the olive oil in a pan. Add the onion, ginger and curry powder. Cook gently for 10 minutes.

2 Add the chopped tomatoes, stock, pomodorino tomatoes and sugar, and season with salt and freshly ground black pepper. Allow to simmer for 10 minutes, stirring occasionally.

3 Add the prawns and simmer for a further 3-5 minutes.

4 Serve the curry on a bed of basmati rice, topped with some crème fraîche or yogurt and a sprinkling of freshly chopped coriander.

**Per serving: 303 cals, 6.7g fat, 3g sat fat, 2.7g total sugars, 1.8g salt**

'Spiced prawns are given
extra flavour with fresh
tomatoes and ginger'

# pasta, rice & noodles

**Serves 4**
Prep time: 15 minutes
Cook time: 40 minutes

# Baked cheese & tomato tortelloni

An easy way to turn a pack of tortelloni into a home-made family meal

1 tablespoon olive oil
1 onion, peeled and roughly chopped
1 x 300g pack Sainsbury's mini Portabella mushrooms, halved
1 x 390g carton Sainsbury's chopped tomatoes with basil & oregano

1 tablespoon tomato purée
1 x 300g pack Sainsbury's spinach & ricotta tortelloni
300g spinach, washed
6 tomatoes, sliced
65g mature Cheddar, grated

1 Preheat the oven to 180°C, fan 160°C, gas 4. Heat the oil in a large frying pan. Add the onion and cook over a medium heat until translucent. Add the mushrooms and continue to fry until the mushrooms have softened. Stir in the chopped tomatoes and tomato purée, season with salt and freshly ground black pepper and set aside.

2 Cook the tortelloni in a large saucepan following pack instructions.

3 Place the spinach in a large colander and drain the cooked pasta over the spinach to wilt it.

4 Return the pasta and wilted spinach to the saucepan and stir through the tomato and mushroom mixture. Pour into a 1.5-litre ovenproof dish and place the tomato slices on the surface so they cover the pasta.

5 Season with salt and freshly ground black pepper, sprinkle with the cheese and bake for 20 minutes.

Per serving: 348 cals, 15.8g fat, 6.7g sat fat, 15.7g total sugars, 1.5g salt

### Wine match
Tomato-based pasta sauces need a crisp white to match the acidity of the tomato, so a delicate Italian white such as Pinot Grigio is perfect

*This cheese bake makes a satisfying and delicious veggie supper*

**Serves 4**
Prep time: 10 minutes
Cook time: 12 minutes

# Mushroom & chilli linguine

This tasty and speedy pasta dish can be on the table in less than 25 minutes

2 tablespoons olive oil
1 onion, peeled and chopped
1 basics red chilli, deseeded and finely sliced
1 x 250g pack Sainsbury's chestnut mushrooms, sliced

1 x 335g pack Sainsbury's cherry tomatoes, halved
½ x 500g pack Sainsbury's linguine
½ x 28g pack Sainsbury's fresh basil, leaves torn
parmesan shavings, to garnish

1  Heat the oil in a wide frying pan. Add the onion and chilli and cook for 5 minutes, then add the mushrooms and cook for a further 3-4 minutes.

2  Add the tomatoes and continue cooking for 2-3 minutes. Meanwhile, cook the linguine until al dente. Drain and toss with the mushroom mixture and basil leaves. Serve sprinkled with parmesan shavings.

Per serving: 324 cals, 8.1g fat, 2g sat fat, 7.2g total sugars, 0.2g salt

**Wine match**
Try a Soave to match this dish, as the zesty freshness will cool the heat from the chilli

**Serves 4**
Prep time: 10 minutes
Cook time: 20 minutes

# Bacon, chilli & pepper pasta

This flavoursome meal uses lots of ingredients from our basics range, making it a great-value meal for any occasion

2 tablespoons olive oil
1 basics red pepper, deseeded and sliced
1 basics yellow pepper, deseeded and sliced
½ x red chilli, deseeded and finely sliced
200g basics unsmoked bacon, sliced into 2cm pieces, fat removed

400g penne
85g basics fresh black pitted olives, halved
1 x 125g pack basics mozzarella cheese ball, torn
handful of fresh basil leaves, to garnish

1  Heat the olive oil in a pan and fry the peppers over a medium heat for about 10 minutes, until the peppers are beginning to soften.

2  Add the chilli and bacon and fry for a further 10 minutes over a medium heat until the bacon juices have evaporated and the bacon begins to brown. Meanwhile, cook the penne following pack instructions.

3  Drain the pasta and add it to the bacon and pepper mixture. Add the olives and mozzarella and stir to combine. Season with salt and freshly ground black pepper and serve with some fresh basil leaves.

Per serving: 643 cals, 23.9g fat, 8.7g sat fat, 8.5g total sugars, 2.7g salt

## Did you know...?
Sainsbury's basics range offers great products at affordable prices. For example, our basics peppers offer the same juicy taste, they're just different sizes

This colourful pasta
dish is packed full
of feisty flavours

**Serves 4**
Prep time: 15 minutes
Cook time: 30 minutes

# Chestnut & sage pasta with pancetta

The saltiness of the pancetta sets off the delicate butternut squash perfectly

1 medium butternut squash, peeled, deseeded and cut into chunks
1 tablespoon olive oil
100g Sainsbury's Italian cubetti di pancetta
1 onion, peeled and chopped
1 red chilli, deseeded and finely chopped

1 tablespoon fresh sage, chopped, plus a few leaves to garnish (optional)
1 x 200g pack Merchant Gourmet whole chestnuts, roughly chopped
1 x 500g pack Sainsbury's fresh pappardelle
1 tablespoon vegetable oil (optional)

1 Preheat the oven to 200°C, fan 180°C, gas 6. Place the butternut squash in a baking tray and toss with the oil. Roast for about 30 minutes, until soft.

2 Meanwhile, dry fry the pancetta in a non-stick pan until crisp, then set aside. In the same pan, fry the onion and chilli until soft. Add the pancetta, sage and chestnuts to the pan and heat through.

3 Cook the pasta following pack instructions. Drain, reserving 100ml cooking water. Stir the squash, chestnuts and reserved cooking water into the pasta. Serve, garnished with sage leaves quickly fried in the vegetable oil, if liked.

Per serving: 487 cals, 16.1g fat, 4.3g sat fat, 13.8g total sugars, 1.3g salt

## Squash & Stilton gnocchi

Preheat the oven to 200°C, fan 180°C, gas 6. Cut 1 peeled and deseeded butternut squash into chunks. Place in a roasting pan with 2 red onions, peeled and cut into crescents, 4 peeled and sliced cloves garlic and 1 tablespoon chopped fresh rosemary. Drizzle with 1 tablespoon olive oil and roast for 30 minutes. Meanwhile, cook 2 x 500g packs Sainsbury's fresh gnocchi, following pack instructions. Drain and toss with 200g Stilton and the squash. Season and serve.

**SERVES 6** Prep time: 15 minutes   Cook time: 30 minutes

**Serves 4**
Prep time: 25 minutes
Cook time: 35 minutes

# Herb meatballs

## with spaghetti & garlic bread

Made with lean mince and fresh herbs, these meatballs coated in tomato sauce are perfect served with pasta

2 tablespoons olive oil

2 onions, peeled and finely chopped

3 cloves garlic, peeled and crushed

3 x 390g cartons Sainsbury's chopped tomatoes in tomato juice

1 tablespoon sugar

1 x 500g pack Sainsbury's extra lean steak mince

1 tablespoon fresh rosemary, finely chopped

1 medium egg, lightly beaten

1 courgette, sliced into rounds and halved

1 red pepper, deseeded and roughly chopped

300g spaghetti

100g mozzarella, torn

1 x 170g pack basics garlic baguette

1 x 70g pack Sainsbury's wild rocket

1 Heat 1 tablespoon olive oil and sauté the onion and garlic for 5 minutes, until soft and golden. Remove a third of the mixture from the pan and set aside to cool. Pour the tomatoes into the pan and stir through the sugar. Cook uncovered for 20 minutes.

2 Meanwhile, mix the minced beef with the reserved, cooled onion and garlic. Add the rosemary and the beaten egg, then divide the mixture into approximately 24 round balls. Heat the remaining 1 tablespoon oil in a frying pan and cook the meatballs for 6-8 minutes, until browned. Once cooked, add the meatballs to the tomato mixture and keep cooking on a low heat while preparing the vegetables.

3 Using the same frying pan, cook the courgette and pepper for 8-10 minutes until soft and lightly charred. Meanwhile, cook the spaghetti following pack instructions.

4 Add the courgette mixture and the mozzarella and spaghetti to the tomato mixture. Stir well to combine and serve with warm garlic bread and a handful of rocket.

Per serving: 841 cals, 27.3g fat, 7.5g sat fat, 27.5g total sugars, 1.5g salt

**Serves 4**
Prep time: 10 minutes
Cook time: 15 minutes

# Broccoli, walnut & chilli pasta

Lemon, chilli and rosemary work together brilliantly in this simple pasta dish, and the walnuts add a savoury crunch

600g broccoli
300g be good to yourself multi-grain fresh tagliatelle
1 tablespoon olive oil, plus extra to drizzle
2 large red chillies, deseeded and finely chopped

3 cloves garlic, peeled and crushed
1 tablespoon fresh rosemary leaves, finely chopped
50g walnut pieces
1 lemon, juice and zest
25g parmesan, finely grated

**1** Cut the broccoli into small florets, then trim the stalks and finely slice. Place all the broccoli in a large pan of boiling water and cook for 8 minutes, then add the tagliatelle and cook for a further 4 minutes. Drain and reserve the cooking liquid.

**2** Meanwhile, heat the olive oil in a large, deep saucepan and gently cook the chilli, garlic and rosemary for 2 minutes. Remove from the heat, add the walnuts, broccoli and pasta and mix well.

**3** Add the lemon juice, zest and some of the reserved pasta water and season with salt and freshly ground black pepper. Divide between 4 plates and serve with a sprinkling of parmesan and a drizzle of extra virgin olive oil.

Per serving: 305 cals, 16.4g fat, 2.6g sat fat, 3.2g total sugars, 0.3g salt

**Love your leftovers**
Toss leftover walnut pieces into your favourite salads for a boost of omega-3, which benefits heart health and brain function

*Walnuts and broccoli add texture to this chilli and herb flavoured pasta*

# Mushroom, thyme & roast chicken risotto

This creamy Italian classic is surprisingly easy to make

½ x 50g pack Sainsbury's dried porcini mushrooms
1 tablespoon olive oil
1 onion, peeled and chopped
1 clove garlic, peeled and chopped
200g chestnut mushrooms, sliced
400g risotto rice (see tips below)
200ml dry white wine, preferably Italian

1.5 litres chicken or vegetable stock (1 stock cube), kept warm on hob
200g cooked chicken, torn into bite-sized pieces
1 tablespoon thyme leaves, plus extra to serve
25g unsalted butter
60g parmesan cheese, plus extra to serve

**1** Cover the porcini mushrooms with boiling water and leave to soak.

**2** Heat the oil in a pan and gently fry the onion for 4 minutes until softened. Add the garlic, stir for 1 minute, then add the chestnut mushrooms and cook, stirring, for 3-4 minutes. Add the rice and stir until the grains are coated in the juices and become translucent. Pour in the wine and stir until completely absorbed.

**3** Ladle in a little stock and stir until almost absorbed. Continue adding the stock a ladleful at a time, stirring continuously, until all the stock is used up or the rice becomes al dente (has a little 'bite' to it). Halfway through cooking, strain the soaked porcini mushrooms, reserving a little of their soaking liquid. Add the mushrooms and the reserved liquid to the risotto.

**4** Add the chicken and thyme 5 minutes before the end of cooking. Stir in the butter and parmesan and season with salt and freshly ground black pepper. Serve garnished with parmesan shavings and thyme.

Per serving: 607 cals, 17.7g fat, 9.7g sat fat, 3g total sugars, 1g salt

## Tips for success
Arborio risotto rice has a large round grain with a lovely creamy texture when cooked. Carnaroli rice is a slightly longer grain that tends to hold its shape better and is a good choice for beginners. Keep stirring your risotto and don't add more liquid until the previous ladleful has been absorbed

Serves 4
Prep time: 15 minutes
Cook time: 25 minutes

# Thai red curry

This is an unusual one-pot Thai red curry, as the rice is cooked in with the rest of the ingredients

2 tablespoons sunflower oil
1 onion, peeled and finely sliced
3 cloves garlic, peeled and finely chopped
4 chicken breasts, cut into chunks
3 tablespoons Sainsbury's Thai red curry paste
200g basmati rice
300ml chicken stock

200ml light coconut milk
100g mange tout
1 yellow pepper, deseeded and sliced
1 x 28g pack Sainsbury's fresh coriander, chopped
1 red chilli, deseeded and finely sliced
lime wedges, to garnish

1 Heat 1 tablespoon oil in a large casserole dish and gently fry the onion and garlic for 5-8 minutes, or until soft. Remove from the pan and set aside.

2 Add the remaining 1 tablespoon oil to the pan and fry the chicken over a high heat for 2-3 minutes until browned all over. Return the onions and garlic to the pan along with the curry paste and rice. Stir well and cook for a further 3 minutes.

3 Stir in the stock and coconut milk, bring to the boil, then cover and simmer for 6-8 minutes. Add the mange tout and pepper and cook for a further 2-3 minutes, or until the rice is cooked through and vegetables are just tender.

4 Stir through the coriander, sprinkle with chilli and serve with wedges of lime.

Per serving: 537 cals, 15.9g fat, 8.8g sat fat, 7.2g total sugars, 1.1g salt

## Love your leftovers
Mix a little leftover Thai red curry paste with yogurt for a marinade for cubed chicken or pork, then cook on skewers for a twist on traditional kebabs

**Serves 4**
Prep time: 10 minutes
Cook time: 10 minutes

# Pad Thai

This spicy mix of prawns, peanuts and garlic is very quick and easy to make

250g thick rice noodles

2 tablespoons groundnut oil

2 x 180g packs Sainsbury's raw peeled king prawns

2 cloves garlic, peeled and finely chopped

1 red chilli, deseeded and finely chopped

2 eggs, lightly beaten

150g fresh beansprouts

3 tablespoons sweet chilli sauce

3 limes, zest and juice

2 tablespoons roasted peanuts, chopped

½ x 28g pack Sainsbury's fresh coriander, chopped

1 lime, cut into wedges, to serve

1  Cook the noodles following pack instructions. Drain and set aside.

2  Heat 1 tablespoon oil in a large frying pan or wok. Add the prawns and stir-fry for 2 minutes until pink. Remove and set aside.

3  Heat the remaining 1 tablespoon oil and fry the garlic and chilli for about 30 seconds. Add the eggs and cook, stirring, for 1 minute. Add the noodles, beansprouts, chilli sauce, lime zest and juice and the prawns. Cook for 2 minutes.

4  Serve sprinkled with peanuts and coriander, with a lime wedge on the side.

Per serving: 338 cals, 15.5g fat, 2.7g sat fat, 10.1g total sugars, 1.7g salt

**Wine match**
Gewürztraminer is great with spicy food, as the delicate sweetness tames the chilli, and the exotic fruit flavours complement the lime and coriander

*A quick and easy
dish that's popular
in Thailand*

**Serves 4**
Prep time: 25 minutes +
15 minutes' marinating
Cook time: 20 minutes

# Pork satay
## with broccoli & spaghetti

These skewers of pork are marinated in a Thai peanut sauce

2 dried kaffir lime leaves, soaked in water
2 tablespoons peanut butter
1 red chilli, deseeded and chopped, plus extra to garnish
2 cloves garlic, peeled and crushed
1 tablespoon fresh grated ginger
1 lime, zest and juice
2 tablespoons light soy sauce, plus extra for seasoning
½ tablespoon light muscovado sugar

½ x 28g pack Sainsbury's fresh coriander, chopped
1 x 500g pack be good to yourself pork medallions, sliced into 2.5cm chunks
150g wholewheat spaghetti
½ tablespoon sunflower oil
1 x 200g pack Sainsbury's tenderstem broccoli, trimmed
25g cashews or peanuts
100ml low-fat plain yogurt

1 To make the satay sauce, drain the lime leaves and finely shred. Place in a blender along with the peanut butter, chilli, garlic, ginger, lime zest and juice, soy sauce, sugar and half the coriander. Blend until smooth.

2 Soak 8 wooden skewers in water. Meanwhile, place the pork chunks in a plastic food bag and add the satay sauce. Seal the bag and then massage the pork to coat the pieces thoroughly. Set aside to marinate for 15 minutes.

3 Preheat the grill to high. Thread the pork pieces onto the wooden skewers and grill for 12-15 minutes, turning occasionally, until cooked through and lightly charred.

4 Meanwhile, cook the spaghetti following pack instructions, then drain and set aside. Heat the oil in a large wok and stir-fry the broccoli and cashews or peanuts for 3-5 minutes. Add the spaghetti, heat through for a couple of minutes, stirring, and season with soy sauce. Keep warm.

5 Add the remaining coriander to the spaghetti and divide between 4 warmed bowls. Top with the pork skewers, garnish with chilli and serve immediately with the yogurt on the side.

**Per serving: 476 cals, 14.3g fat, 2.8g sat fat, 5.5g total sugars, 1.3g salt**

# desserts

desserts

**Serves 8**
Prep time: 30 minutes,
plus 1–2 hours to chill
Cook time: 15 minutes

# Coconut meringue roulade
## with passion fruit cream

This impressive dessert is perfect for a special occasion

3 large egg whites
225g caster sugar
100g desiccated coconut
1 x 300ml pot Sainsbury's double cream
zest of 1 lime, plus extra to decorate
4 passion fruit, halved and seeds scooped out

200ml crème fraîche
1 tablespoon lime juice
1½ tablespoons icing sugar, sifted
1 Sainsbury's Fairtrade pineapple, peeled, cored and cut into slices

1  Preheat the oven to 180°C, fan 160°C, gas 4. Line a 22 x 32cm baking tray with baking parchment.

2  To make the meringue, whisk together the egg whites until they become glossy with stiff peaks, then slowly pour in the sugar, whisking continuously until the mixture again becomes stiff and glossy. Spread into the tin.

3  Sprinkle the coconut over the meringue then bake for 15 minutes, or until the top is becoming golden and the meringue is puffed. Remove from the oven and leave to cool in the tin for 5 minutes, then turn out onto a sheet of baking parchment, coconut-side down. Leave to cool for a further 10 minutes while you make the filling.

4  Whip the cream with the lime zest until soft peaks are formed, then stir in the passion fruit pulp. Stir to combine then mix in the crème fraîche, lime juice and icing sugar. Spread over the meringue, then use the baking parchment to help you roll up the roulade. Keeping it wrapped in the baking parchment, leave for 1–2 hours in the fridge to set.

5  Just before serving, heat a griddle pan over a high heat and sear the pineapple slices for a minute on each side. Place in a bowl and garnish with strips of lime zest. Cut the roulade into slices at the table and serve with the caramelised pineapple.

**Per serving:** 492 cals, 33.5g fat, 24.3g sat fat, 43.9g total sugars, trace salt

**Serves 6**
Prep time: 20 minutes
Cook time: 35 minutes

# Cinnamon, pear & stem ginger pudding

These attractive puds are full of warming seasonal flavours

175g unsalted butter
175g light soft brown sugar
3 eggs
175g self-raising flour
1 teaspoon baking powder
½ teaspoon ground cinnamon

3 pieces stem ginger, finely chopped, plus 3 tablespoons stem ginger syrup
6 very ripe small pears, peeled and cored with an apple corer or melon baller
icing sugar, to dust

1  Preheat the oven to 190°C, fan 170°C, gas 5.

2  Cream the butter and sugar together with an electric whisk until pale. Beat in the eggs one at a time. Sift over the flour, baking powder and cinnamon and fold in until well combined. Add the stem ginger and stir well. Divide the mixture between 6 deep, heat-proof pudding bowls or cappuccino cups (about 300ml capacity).

3  Push a pear into the centre of each pudding and bake for 35 minutes, until the mixture has risen around the pears. Dust with icing sugar and drizzle the stem ginger syrup over the pears, then serve.

**Per serving: 546 cals, 27.5g fat, 16.7g sat fat, 45.8g total sugars, 0.6g salt**

Tips for success
If your pears are hard, poach them in water for 8–10 minutes, then drain well and pat dry with kitchen paper and they'll be ready to use in the recipe. You can also use tinned pears – they're equally delicious. Simply chop and pop into the bottom of the bowls or cups, then cover with the sponge mixture

*These sponge puds are baked with fresh pears and stem ginger*

**Serves 6**
Prep time: 20 minutes
Cook time: 1 hour

# Easiest apple tart

This apple tart looks and tastes amazing but is simple to make. Filled with a gorgeous frangipane mixture, it's a real crowd pleaser

80g butter
80g caster sugar
1 egg and 1 egg yolk
100g ground almonds

25g plain flour
1 x 240g Sainsbury's sweet pastry case
1 large Bramley apple, cored and thinly sliced
apricot jam, melted, to glaze

1  Preheat the oven to 180°C, fan 160°C, gas 4. Cream together the butter, sugar, egg and yolk, almonds and flour. Pour into the pastry case.

2  Quarter and thinly slice the apple. Lay the slices in concentric circles, working towards the centre. Continue to add layers of overlapping slices until all the apple slices are used. Bake for 1 hour. Glaze with the melted jam and serve either hot or cold.

**Per serving: 499 cals, 32.9g fat, 12.4g sat fat, 19.2g total sugars, trace salt**

## Apple pancakes

Mix 300g self-raising flour with 25g soft brown sugar. Whisk 2 large egg yolks with 400ml Sainsbury's buttermilk. Beat into the flour until smooth, and set aside for 10 minutes. Whisk 2 large egg whites with a pinch of salt until soft peaks form. Beat a large spoonful into the flour mixture, then fold in the rest. Heat a little oil in a non-stick pan and add large spoonfuls of batter. Press a thin slice of apple into each and cook for 2–3 minutes on each side. Serve with maple syrup.

**SERVES 4** Prep time: 10 minutes  Cook time: 18 minutes

**desserts**

**Serves 4**
Prep time: 10 minutes
Cook time: 5 minutes

# Chocolate espresso ripple pots

A decadent combination of coffee and chocolate - for best results, make these puds at least 30 minutes ahead to allow the flavours to mingle

6 Taste the Difference almond & chocolate biscotti
4 tablespoons freshly made espresso or strong fresh coffee
50g Green & Black's Maya Gold chocolate, broken into chunks

75ml double cream
4 tablespoons Baileys or Taste the Difference Irish Cream Liqueur
100g mascarpone

1 Break the biscuits into rough pieces and divide between 4 coffee cups or glasses (they must have a capacity of 125ml). Pour over the espresso.

2 Melt the chocolate either in a heat-proof bowl set over a pan of simmering water or in the microwave.

3 Beat together the double cream, Baileys and mascarpone until smooth and creamy. Pour over the melted chocolate and stir a couple of times until rippled. Spoon over the biscuits and serve.

Per serving: 305 cals, 25.6g fat, 13.4g sat fat, 6g total sugars, trace salt

**Try something new...**
For a different twist on these little chocolate pots, you can vary the liqueur – Tia Maria or Kahlúa work as well as Irish Cream

desserts

**Serves 8**
Prep time: 15 minutes
Cook time: 30 minutes

# Mango & ginger crumble

Mango and raspberries make a more unusual filling for this family favourite, which is sprinkled with flaked almonds for an enticing crumble topping

100g unsalted butter, diced, plus extra
for greasing
3 basics mangoes, peeled, stoned and
chopped into 3cm cubes
250g frozen raspberries
1 teaspoon freshly grated ginger

100g fresh breadcrumbs
100g whole rolled porridge oats
100g golden caster sugar, plus an extra
½ tablespoon for sprinkling
25g flaked almonds

1  Preheat the oven to 200°C, fan 180°C, gas 6.

2  Grease a baking dish with butter. Place the mango cubes, raspberries and ginger in the dish.

3  Pour the breadcrumbs into a mixing bowl and stir in the oats. Add the butter and use your fingertips to work it into a crumble. Stir through the sugar.

4  Spoon the crumble over the fruit mixture and sprinkle on the flaked almonds and extra sugar. Bake for 30 minutes until golden. Great served with hot custard.

**Per serving: 311 cals, 13.5g fat, 7.2g sat fat, 25.7g total sugars, 0.3g salt**

**Did you know...?**
Sainsbury's sells a large range of frozen fruits, including raspberries, blueberries and cherries. They're ideal for quick and easy desserts

Serves 12
Prep time: 1 hour
Cook time: 1 hour

# Sticky toffee pud
## with whiskey caramel sauce

Your best-ever sticky toffee pudding! The Irish whiskey gives this an amazing twist - for a child-friendly version, substitute the whiskey for apple juice

**FOR THE WHISKEY CARAMEL SAUCE**
325ml double cream
125g brown sugar
35g unsalted butter
50ml Irish whiskey

**FOR THE PUDDING**
200ml Irish whiskey

150g dates, pitted and roughly chopped
2 teaspoons bicarbonate of soda
250g plain flour
2 teaspoons baking powder
225g unsalted butter, at room temperature
180g granulated sugar
4 medium eggs
2 teaspoons vanilla extract

1 Combine all the whiskey caramel sauce ingredients in a large, heavy-bottomed pot. Bring to the boil, stirring constantly, then reduce the heat to a simmer. Continue to cook for 15 minutes, or until the sauce has reduced by half.

2 Preheat the oven to 180°C, fan 160°C, gas 4. Grease a 20cm round cake tin. Place the whiskey, dates and bicarbonate of soda in a medium saucepan. Bring to the boil, then remove from the heat and allow to cool completely. In a separate bowl, mix the flour and baking powder together.

3 Using an electric mixer, beat the butter and sugar together in another bowl for 3-4 minutes, until light and fluffy, then beat in the eggs one at a time. Add the vanilla and half the flour mixture. Mix in the cooled date and whiskey mixture and the remainder of the flour mixture until well blended. Pour into the cake tin and bake for 45 minutes.

4 Remove from the oven. Use a skewer to poke numerous holes into the top of the pud, then pour up to half the whiskey caramel sauce over the top. Bake for another 15 minutes, or until a skewer inserted into it comes out clean. (Place a baking sheet in the bottom of the oven to catch any syrup drips.) Remove from the oven and allow to cool in the tin for 10 minutes.

5 Invert onto a plate and serve with the remaining warm whiskey caramel sauce. Great with cream or custard.

**Per serving: 507 cals, 33g fat, 20.4g sat fat, 31.2g total sugars, 0.7g salt**

‘ Dripping with a rich sauce, this date-filled pudding is such a treat ’

**Serves 4**
Prep time: 15 minutes
Cook time: 30 minutes

# Cinnamon & red wine poached fruit

The red-wine sauce becomes almost syrupy in this fabulously fruity dessert

1 x 75cl bottle basics red wine
200g caster sugar
1 cinnamon stick

3 basics pears, peeled and sliced
2 peaches, stoned and quartered
4 basics plums, stoned and halved

1 Pour the wine into a large saucepan. Add the sugar and cinnamon, then cover and bring to the boil. Simmer for 5 minutes, until the sugar has dissolved.

2 Add the fruit, then cover and simmer for 10 minutes. Remove the lid and simmer for a further 10 minutes, until the fruit is tender and the liquid has reduced slightly. Great served with natural yogurt.

**Per serving: 302 cals, 0.2g fat, 0g sat fat, 73.6g total sugars, trace salt**

## Blackberry puddings

Preheat the oven to 200ºC, fan 180ºC, gas 6. In a bowl, sprinkle 150g blackberries with 1 tablespoon each caster sugar and crème de cassis. Set aside. Sift 100g self-raising flour into a large bowl. Rub in 50g butter until it resembles fine breadcrumbs. Stir in 85g caster sugar and 150ml semi-skimmed milk. Divide the berries between 4 ramekins, discarding the juices. Top with the batter. Bake on a baking tray for 30-40 minutes. Serve dusted with a little icing sugar.

**SERVES 4** Prep time: 15 minutes  Cook time: 40 minutes

**Serves 4**
Prep time: 10 minutes
Cook time: 28 minutes

# Meringue-topped baked apples

These impressive-looking desserts are surprisingly easy to make

75g raisins
½ teaspoon ground cinnamon
½ teaspoon ground mixed spice
3 tablespoons runny honey

4 Cox's apples
1 medium egg white
50g caster sugar

1 Preheat the oven to 200°C, fan 180°C, gas 6. In a small bowl, mix together the raisins, spices and honey. Set aside.

2 Core the apples, then score around the middle of each. Place in a baking dish and pack the raisin mixture into the centre of each. Bake for 25 minutes until the apples are just soft, then remove and set aside.

3 Increase the oven temperature to 240°C, fan 220°C, gas 9. In a bowl, whisk the egg white to stiff peaks. Gradually whisk in the sugar, until you have a glossy meringue.

4 Transfer the meringue to a piping bag fitted with a fluted nozzle. Pipe generously onto each apple, in a spiral. Bake for 3 minutes, or until the meringue is golden. Serve hot.

**Per serving: 177 cals, 0.2g fat, 0g sat fat, 42.1g total sugars, trace salt**

'Raisin-filled apple and golden meringue work together beautifully here'

**Serves 6**
Prep time: 15 minutes
Cook time: 12 minutes

# Chocolate pots

These gorgeous chocolate puds have a secret truffle centre...

150g unsalted butter, plus extra
for greasing
150g caster sugar, plus extra for coating
150g Taste the Difference Belgian dark
chocolate

3 large eggs
50g plain flour, sifted
6 x Taste the Difference Belgian
flaked truffles

1  Preheat the oven to 200°C, fan 180°C, gas 6.

2  Lightly grease 6 x 150ml ramekins with butter. Fill each with caster sugar, rotate until fully coated with sugar, then empty.

3  Over a very low heat, melt the chocolate and butter together, stirring occasionally, then set aside to cool slightly.

4  Gradually whisk the sugar into the eggs until pale and thick. Stir the melted chocolate into the egg mixture, then fold in the flour.

5  Spoon half the mixture into the ramekins, drop a truffle into the middle of each one, then top with the remaining mixture. Transfer to a baking tray and bake for 10-12 minutes, or until each is risen and coming away from the edges. Great served with double cream.

**Per serving: 438 cals, 28.8g fat, 17.6g sat fat, 32.3g total sugars, 0.1g salt**

**Serves 8**
Prep time: 10 minutes
Chilling time: 1 hour

**V**

# No-bake blueberry cheesecake

With a delicious gooey topping, this cheesecake is so easy to make. Made with lots of ingredients from Sainsbury's basics range, it's also a great-value dessert

100g basics butter, melted
200g basics digestive biscuits, crushed into fine crumbs
3 x 200g packs basics soft cheese
150g icing sugar
2 teaspoons vanilla extract

zest of 2 basics lemons
1 x 300ml pot Sainsbury's double cream

**FOR THE COMPOTE**
1 x 125g pack basics blueberries
1 teaspoon basics honey

1 Mix together the butter and biscuits. Spoon into a 23cm springform cake tin lined with baking parchment. Flatten firmly to ensure there are no cracks, then refrigerate.

2 Prepare the filling by beating the soft cheese with the icing sugar until well combined. Add the vanilla extract, then stir in the lemon zest and cream until well combined.

3 Pour the mixture into the tin and refrigerate for 1 hour. Meanwhile, to make the compote, gently simmer the blueberries with the honey until the berries start to burst. Pour over the cheesecake to serve.

**Per serving: 661 cals, 51.8g fat, 32.5g sat fat, 27.9g total sugars, 1.1g salt**

'Quick to prepare, this cheesecake is the perfect dinner-party dessert'

**Serves 6**
Prep time: 20 minutes
Cook time: 45 minutes

# Cherry clafoutis

This easy French dessert of fruit baked in batter is great with ice cream

75g unsalted butter
120g caster sugar, plus extra for dusting
pinch of salt
50g plain flour
50g ground almonds
1 medium egg, plus 3 egg yolks

1 teaspoon vanilla extract
200ml semi-skimmed milk
100ml double cream
1 x 425g tin Sainsbury's pitted black
cherries in fruit juice
icing sugar, to dust

1  Melt the butter in the microwave, or over a low heat, then allow to cool.
   Preheat the oven to 190°C, fan 170°C, gas 5.

2  Brush the inside of a 1-litre baking dish with a little of the melted butter,
   then dust with caster sugar.

3  Using an electric whisk, mix the sugar, salt, flour, almonds, egg, yolks and
   vanilla extract in a large bowl. Slowly add the milk, cream and melted
   butter, continuing to whisk.

4  Drain the cherries and discard the juice. Add the cherries to the batter mix,
   then pour into the baking dish. Bake for 45 minutes, until set. Serve warm,
   dusted with icing sugar.

**Per serving: 499 cals, 32.1g fat, 14.9g sat fat, 31.8g total sugars, 0.5g salt**

**Serves 8**
Prep time: 15 minutes,
plus 35 minutes to stand
Cook time: 35 minutes

**V**

# Spiced pear bread & butter pudding

Mincemeat and pear add seasonal flavours to this classic pud

60g unsalted butter
6-8 slices white bread, crusts removed
4 tablespoons mincemeat
2 ripe red pears, cored and thickly sliced
1 tablespoon demerara sugar

**FOR THE CUSTARD**
25g caster sugar
300ml milk
1 x 300ml pot Sainsbury's double cream
3 medium eggs, beaten

1 Preheat the oven to 180°C, fan 160°C, gas 4. Butter the bread on one side. Spread the mincemeat onto the bread, then cut into triangles and arrange in a 2-litre ovenproof dish. Tuck the pears between the slices.

2 Beat together the custard ingredients, strain and pour over the bread and pears. Sprinkle over the demerara sugar and allow to stand for 20 minutes. Bake for 30-35 minutes, or until the custard is just set.

3 Remove from the oven and allow to stand for a further 15 minutes, then serve. Great with cream.

Per serving: 424 cals, 27.8g fat, 16.3g sat fat, 13.9g total sugars, 0.6g salt

**Makes 12**
Prep time: 30 minutes
Cook time: 20 minutes

# Chocolate & almond cupcakes

Ground almonds boost the flavour of these wonderfully moist cupcakes

60g unsalted butter, softened
125g granulated sugar
1 large egg
100g self-raising flour
30g cocoa powder
60g ground almonds
100ml semi-skimmed milk

FOR THE VANILLA BUTTERCREAM ICING
150g unsalted butter, softened
1 teaspoon vanilla extract
250g icing sugar
30g flaked almonds, toasted

1 Preheat the oven to 180°C, fan 160°C, gas 4. In a large bowl, beat the butter with the sugar until light and fluffy. Whisk in the egg.

2 In a separate bowl, sift together the flour and cocoa and stir in the ground almonds. Add to the sugar, butter and egg mixture and stir to combine. Add the milk gradually until well combined.

3 Use scissors to cut 12 squares of baking parchment, then line the holes of a muffin tin. Spoon the cake mixture into each casing and bake for 20 minutes, or until a skewer inserted into the cakes comes out clean. Leave to cool on a wire rack.

4 While the cakes are baking, make the buttercream icing. Cream the butter together with the vanilla extract. Sift in the icing sugar and whisk until light and creamy.

5 When the cakes are cool, spoon the icing into a piping bag and pipe generous swirls on top of each cake. Sprinkle with toasted flaked almonds.

Per serving: 356 cals, 19.9g fat, 10.4g sat fat, 33.5g total sugars, 0.2g salt

Serves 12
Prep time: 30 minutes,
plus 10 minutes' cooling
Cook time: 45 minutes

# Decadent chocolate cake

A wicked combination of chocolate and raspberries creates the ultimate cake

75g cocoa powder
4 medium eggs
1 teaspoon vanilla extract
300g self-raising flour, plus extra for dusting
4 teaspoons baking powder
½ teaspoon salt
400g caster sugar
50ml sunflower oil

225g unsalted butter, softened, plus extra for greasing

FOR THE GANACHE
2 tablespoons golden syrup
125g caster sugar
2 x 100g packs Taste the Difference Belgian dark chocolate, broken into small pieces
170g raspberries

1  Preheat the oven to 180°C, fan 160°C, gas 4. Grease 2 x 23cm cake tins and dust well with flour. Pour the cocoa into a bowl. Add 200ml boiling water and stir until smooth.

2  Gently whisk the eggs with the vanilla and 90ml water until combined, then set aside.

3  In a separate bowl, sieve the flour with the baking powder, salt and sugar. Add the cocoa mixture and the oil and butter. Beat for 1 minute using an electric whisk. Gradually add the egg mixture, whisking well after each addition.

4  Divide the mixture between the prepared cake tins. Bake for 40-45 minutes, or until a skewer inserted into the cake comes out clean. Leave to cool in the tins for 10 minutes, then transfer to a cooling rack.

5  When the cake is almost cool, make the ganache. In a saucepan, heat the golden syrup with the sugar and 60ml water, stirring occasionally to dissolve the sugar. Once dissolved, bring to the boil then remove from the heat. Add the chocolate, then leave to melt. Stir until glossy and thick.

6  Spread a third of the ganache over one sponge. Add two thirds of the raspberries, then top with the other sponge. Pour over the remaining ganache, letting it dribble over the sides. Decorate with the remaining raspberries.

**Per serving: 598 cals, 28.8g fat, 15.5g sat fat, 57.5g total sugars, 1g salt**

**Serves 12**
Prep time: 20 minutes
Cook time: 1 hour

# Banana cake
## with butterscotch drizzle

Butterscotch complements banana beautifully in this moreish cake

175g plain flour, plus extra for dusting

2 teaspoons baking powder

½ teaspoon bicarbonate of soda

125g unsalted butter, melted, plus extra for greasing

150g golden caster sugar

2 large eggs

4 small, very ripe bananas, peeled and mashed

75g walnut halves, chopped

1 teaspoon vanilla extract

banana coins, to decorate

**FOR THE BUTTERSCOTCH DRIZZLE**

75g golden caster sugar

15g unsalted butter

50g light muscovado sugar

1 tablespoon golden syrup

75ml double cream

1   Preheat the oven to 180°C, fan 160°C, gas 4.

2   Grease an 8cm deep, 25 x 10cm loaf tin and dust with flour. In a bowl, mix together the flour, baking powder and bicarbonate of soda.

3   In a separate bowl, mix the butter and sugar with an electric hand mixer. Beat in the eggs one at a time, then add the bananas, walnuts and vanilla extract. Gradually add the flour mixture, stirring well.

4   Pour into the greased loaf tin and bake on the centre shelf of the oven for 50-60 minutes, or until a skewer inserted into the cake comes out clean. Leave in the tin to cool.

5   Meanwhile, place all the butterscotch drizzle ingredients in a saucepan and simmer over a low heat for 5-7 minutes, until smooth and dark golden. Leave to thicken and cool slightly, then pour over the cake and decorate with the banana coins.

**Per serving: 363 cals, 18.8g fat, 8.9g sat fat, 27.6g total sugars, 0.4g salt**

# Christmas

**Serves 10**
Prep time: 45 minutes
Cook time: 4 hours,
plus 30 minutes to rest

# Festive roast turkey

Served with delicious stuffing balls, this traditional roast tastes as impressive as it looks, topped with a latticework of crisp bacon

125g unsalted butter, softened

1 heaped tablespoon thyme leaves

1 x 20g pack Sainsbury's fresh sage, finely chopped, with extra to garnish

2 cloves garlic, peeled and finely chopped

1 x 5kg free-range turkey

1 x 240g pack Taste the Difference smoked streaky bacon rashers

**FOR THE STUFFING BALLS**

500g Sainsbury's Butcher's Choice pork sausagemeat

45g fresh white breadcrumbs

140g chestnuts, peeled, chopped and cooked

20g Sainsbury's fresh flat-leaf parsley, finely chopped

1 onion, peeled and finely chopped

zest of $1/2$ a lemon

$1/4$ teaspoon ground cloves

1 free-range egg, beaten

1  Preheat the oven to 200°C, fan 180°C, gas 6. In a bowl, mix together the butter, thyme, sage and garlic, and season well with salt and pepper.

2  Being careful not to tear the skin, use your fingertips to separate the turkey skin from the breast meat. Push in the herb butter and spread evenly over the breast. Lay the bacon over the breast, overlapping as you do so.

3  Tie the turkey legs together with string and place the bird on a rack inside a large roasting tin. Roast for 30 minutes, uncovered, then remove from the oven and loosely cover with buttered foil. Reduce the temperature to 180°C, fan 160°C, gas 4. Continue roasting for 3-3$1/2$ hours, basting every 45 minutes with the juices, until cooked through. Remove the foil a few minutes before the end of cooking if the skin still needs to crisp up.

4  Mix all the stuffing ingredients together and season. Shape into 20 balls and place in the oven in a roasting tin, 25 minutes before the turkey has finished cooking.

5  To test whether the turkey is cooked, insert a skewer into the thickest part of the leg - the juices should run clear. Transfer to a warmed serving plate, cover loosely with foil and leave to rest for 30 minutes before carving. Garnish with the sage leaves and serve with the stuffing balls.

Per serving: 484 cals, 27.3g fat, 12.6g sat fat, 2.2g total sugars, 1.7g salt

# Side dishes

## Perfect roasties

100g goose fat

2kg King Edward potatoes, peeled

1 teaspoon sea salt

4 sprigs of rosemary, leaves only, chopped

1 Preheat the oven to 220°C, fan 200°C, gas 7. Place the goose fat in a large roasting tin and heat in the oven for 10 minutes or until sizzling hot.

2 Meanwhile, cut the potatoes into chunks. Cover with cold water in a large pan. Add a pinch of salt, bring to the boil, then simmer for 10-12 minutes to parboil. Drain, then return to the pan. Cook, covered, over a low heat for 1-2 minutes, then shake the pan to fluff up the edges, and season with the sea salt.

3 Carefully spoon the potatoes into the hot tin, turning to coat. Sprinkle with the rosemary. Roast for 30-40 minutes, turning occasionally, until crisp and golden.

Per serving: 246 cals, 10.5g fat, 3.3g sat fat, 0.8g total sugars, 0.5g salt

SERVES 10   Prep time: 15 minutes   Cook time: 40 minutes

## Sprouts with pancetta & hazelnuts

600g sprouts, trimmed

25g unsalted butter

1 tablespoon olive oil

100g shallots, peeled and sliced

1 x 206g pack Sainsbury's Simply Italian cubetti di pancetta

sprig of thyme, leaves only

50g blanched hazelnuts, roughly chopped

1 Boil the sprouts for 3-4 minutes, until tender but firm. Drain and run under cold water. Lay on a tea towel to absorb excess water.

2 Melt the butter and olive oil in a large, heavy-based frying pan. Gently cook the shallots for 5 minutes, then add the pancetta and thyme. Cook for another 10 minutes, until beginning to crisp. Add the hazelnuts and sprouts to the pan, fry over a high heat for 2-3 minutes to heat through, then serve.

Per serving: 268 cals, 22.4g fat, 7.2g sat fat, 4.2g total sugars, 1.4g salt

SERVES 6   Prep time: 15 minutes   Cook time: 20 minutes

Serves 6
Prep time: 20 minutes
Cook time: 10 minutes
in microwave
(or 4 hours' steaming)

# Christmas pudding

Packed with flavour, this fruity, festive pud is quick and easy to cook

50g fresh wholemeal breadcrumbs
1 egg, beaten
50g self-raising flour, sifted
1 level teaspoon mixed spice
200g Sainsbury's luxury mixed dried fruit

225g mincemeat
2 tablespoons semi-skimmed milk
2 level tablespoons dark treacle
4 tablespoons brandy, to serve
brandy butter, to serve (see below)

1  Place all the ingredients (except the brandy and brandy butter) in a large bowl and mix well. Spoon into a greased 600ml pudding basin and cover with cling film. Microwave on high for 10 minutes.

2  To serve, pour on the brandy, warmed in a pan, and top with brandy butter.

Per serving: 288 cals, 2.4g fat, 1g sat fat, 47.6g total sugars, 0.3g salt

**Prefer steaming?** Instead of cling film, cover the basin with greased baking parchment and then a layer of foil, tucking the edges around the rim. Place on an upturned saucer in a saucepan and add hot water to halfway up the basin. Bring to the boil and keep the water on a gentle boil, checking regularly - add water so it doesn't boil dry. Steam for 4 hours. Serve as above. Alternatively, keep the pudding in the basin in a cool place for up to 1 week and steam again for 1 hour before serving.

## Cinnamon-spiced brandy butter

Whizz 50g soft, unsalted butter and 150g light soft brown sugar together in a food processor until smooth, then add ½ teaspoon cinnamon and pulse to combine. Add 5 tablespoons brandy, 1 tablespoon at a time, pulsing between each addition until smooth and thick. Transfer to a bowl and chill. Take some paper, cut out a star, then place the stencil over the bowl. Dust with cinnamon to create the star effect, and serve with your Christmas pud.

**SERVES 10**  Prep time: 10 minutes

Serves 25
Prep time: 30 minutes
Cook time: 3 hours,
plus cooling time

# Christmas cake

A traditional fruit-rich cake that's delicious at any time of year

800g Sainsbury's luxury mixed fruit
5 tablespoons brandy
2 balls stem ginger, finely chopped
50g blanched almonds, chopped
zest of 1 lemon and 1 orange
175g plain flour
1 teaspoon ground mixed spice
1 teaspoon ground cinnamon
225g dark muscovado sugar

225g unsalted butter
4 medium eggs, beaten
50g ground almonds
3 tablespoons apricot glaze, warmed
icing sugar, for dusting
1 x 454g pack Sainsbury's gold marzipan
750g Sainsbury's ready to roll icing
red sugar balls from Sainsbury's decorating
kit, and holly & ivy cake decoration

1 Preheat the oven to 160°C, fan 140°C, gas 3. Grease an 18cm square cake
   tin and line with baking parchment. Tie a folded piece of baking parchment
   around the outside of the tin to protect against the heat.

2 Place the mixed fruit and brandy in a large pan and heat gently for 4
   minutes. Transfer to a bowl and leave to cool (the fruit will soak up the
   brandy). Add the ginger, chopped almonds and orange and lemon zest.

3 Sift the flour, spices and ½ teaspoon salt into another bowl. In a separate
   large bowl, whisk together the sugar and butter until fluffy, then gradually
   beat in the eggs until combined. Fold in the flour and spice mixture and
   the ground almonds, then fold in the soaked fruit and nut mixture.

4 Spoon into the prepared tin and level. Bake for 2½-3 hours, until a skewer
   inserted into the middle comes out clean. Cover with foil if it's getting too dark.
   Leave to cool in the tin for a few minutes, then transfer to a cooling rack.

5 Brush the cake with the glaze. On a little icing sugar, roll out the marzipan
   to ½cm thick. Lay over the cake, trim, then brush with boiled, cooled water.
   Roll out the icing to 1cm thick, then lay over the cake and trim.

6 Cut 3 stars from the icing trimmings with a large cookie cutter. Remove the
   centres with a smaller star cutter and set aside. Stick the outlines on the cake
   with warm water. Brush inside them with a little water and fill with sugar balls.
   Stick on smaller stars with warm water and add the cake decoration.

Per serving: 314 cals, 13g fat, 5.5g sat fat, 72.7g total sugars, 0.2g salt

# Find the right recipe at a glance

## No more than 5 ingredients

| | |
|---|---|
| Apple pancakes | 154 |
| Cheesy cabbage & potato wraps | 82 |
| Chorizo, red pepper, butter bean & spinach salad | 26 |
| Cinnamon-spiced brandy butter | 186 |
| Creamy root vegetable mash | 82 |
| Crushed minty peas | 120 |
| Garlicky carrots | 84 |
| Juicy apricot chicken | 66 |
| Mozzarella & bacon stuffed aubergine | 86 |
| Pecan-crusted duck | 68 |
| Perfect roasties | 184 |
| Sesame tuna & chips | 120 |
| Spicy sweet potato wedges | 88 |
| Steamed broccoli with toasted sesame seeds | 84 |
| Stir-fried chilli Savoy cabbage | 86 |

## Ⓥ Vegetarian

| | |
|---|---|
| Baked cheese & tomato tortelloni | 128 |
| Broccoli & Stilton soup with Cheddar toasts | 10 |
| Broccoli, walnut & chilli pasta | 138 |
| Butternut squash & mozzarella salad | 24 |
| Carrot & cumin soup | 10 |
| Cheesy cabbage & potato wraps | 82 |
| Chick pea salad with pitta croutons | 22 |
| Chicory, walnut & Roquefort salad | 32 |
| Creamy mushrooms on toast | 104 |
| Creamy root vegetable mash | 82 |
| Crushed minty peas | 120 |
| Cumin & coriander potato fritters | 88 |
| Garlicky carrots | 84 |
| Melanzane alla Parmigiana | 98 |
| Moroccan red lentil & tomato soup | 18 |
| Moroccan-style aubergine salad | 36 |
| Mushroom & chilli linguine | 130 |
| Mushroom & parsley soup | 16 |
| Parsnip, potato & spinach gratin | 80 |
| Pumpkin, sweet potato & red pepper soup | 8 |
| Ratatouille & garlic bread cobbler | 114 |
| Spanakopita lasagne | 56 |
| Spicy sweet potato wedges | 88 |
| Squash & rosemary pasta bake | 60 |
| Squash & Stilton gnocchi | 134 |
| Steamed broccoli with toasted sesame seeds | 84 |
| Stir-fried chilli Savoy cabbage | 86 |
| Sweet potato chilli | 94 |
| Tomato & basil soup with garlic ciabatta | 14 |
| Veggie mushroom nut roast | 76 |
| Veggie sausage, butternut squash & red pepper salad | 34 |
| Warm lentil & avocado salad | 30 |

## ④⑤ On the table in 45 minutes or less

| | |
|---|---|
| Apple pancakes | 154 |
| Bacon & mushroom pasta bake | 58 |
| Bacon, chilli & pepper pasta | 132 |
| Braised celery with bacon & courgettes | 90 |
| Broccoli & Stilton soup with Cheddar toasts | 10 |
| Broccoli, walnut & chilli pasta | 138 |
| Cheesy cabbage & potato wraps | 82 |
| Chestnut & sage pasta with pancetta | 134 |
| Chick pea salad with pitta croutons | 22 |
| Chicory, walnut & Roquefort salad | 32 |
| Chocolate espresso ripple pots | 156 |
| Chocolate pots | 166 |
| Chorizo, red pepper, butter bean & spinach salad | 26 |
| Cinnamon & red wine poached fruit | 162 |
| Cinnamon-spiced brandy butter | 186 |
| Cranberry & Brie stuffed chicken | 100 |
| Creamy mushrooms on toast | 104 |
| Creamy root vegetable mash | 82 |
| Crushed minty peas | 120 |
| Cumin & coriander potato fritters | 88 |
| Ginger & quinoa chicken salad | 32 |
| Hot potato salad with mackerel, rocket & avocado | 28 |
| Individual salmon pie fillet | 52 |
| Mango & ginger crumble | 158 |
| Meringue-topped baked apples | 164 |
| Moroccan-style aubergine salad | 36 |
| Mushroom & chilli linguine | 130 |
| Mushroom & parsley soup | 16 |
| Mushroom, thyme & roast chicken risotto | 140 |
| Pad Thai | 144 |
| Pancetta-wrapped salmon with herby lentils | 122 |
| Pear, walnut & Dolcelatte salad | 38 |
| Pecan-crusted duck | 68 |
| Prawn & tomato curry | 124 |
| Sausage & mash with red onion sauce | 96 |
| Smoky potato salad | 28 |
| Spicy sweet potato wedges | 88 |
| Sprouts with pancetta & hazelnuts | 184 |
| Squash & rosemary pasta bake | 60 |
| Squash & Stilton gnocchi | 134 |
| Steamed broccoli with toasted sesame seeds | 84 |
| Stir-fried chilli Savoy cabbage | 86 |
| Sweet potato chilli | 94 |
| Thai green curry mussel & prawn pot | 116 |
| Thai red curry | 142 |
| Warm lentil & avocado salad | 30 |
| Warm mushroom & bacon salad | 38 |

## Special occasions

| | |
|---|---|
| Braised celery with bacon & courgettes | 90 |
| Cheesy cabbage & potato wraps | 82 |
| Chicory, walnut & Roquefort salad | 32 |
| Chocolate & almond cupcakes | 174 |
| Chocolate espresso ripple pots | 156 |
| Chocolate pots | 166 |
| Cinnamon & red wine poached fruit | 162 |
| Cinnamon, pear & stem ginger pudding | 152 |
| Cranberry & Brie stuffed chicken | 100 |
| Creamy mussel soup | 12 |
| Decadent chocolate cake | 176 |
| Luxury three-fish pie with spinach | 52 |
| Melanzane alla Parmigiana | 98 |
| Mozzarella & bacon stuffed aubergine | 86 |
| Mushroom, thyme & roast chicken risotto | 140 |
| Pancetta-wrapped salmon with herby lentils | 122 |
| Red-wine braised lamb shanks with thyme & rosemary | 104 |
| Thai green curry mussel & prawn pot | 116 |
| Warm mushroom & bacon salad | 38 |

## Family favourites

| | |
|---|---|
| Bacon & mushroom pasta bake | 58 |
| Baked cheese & tomato tortelloni | 128 |
| Banana cake with butterscotch drizzle | 178 |
| Beef brisket pot roast | 72 |
| Broccoli & Stilton soup with Cheddar toasts | 10 |
| Carrot & cumin soup | 10 |
| Cherry clafoutis | 170 |
| Chunky beef casserole | 112 |
| Cider roast pork with mincemeat stuffing | 74 |
| Comforting beef bourguignon pie | 48 |
| Easiest apple tart | 154 |
| Herb meatballs with spaghetti & garlic bread | 136 |
| Indian-spiced shepherd's pie | 102 |
| Individual salmon fillet pie | 52 |
| Lamb moussaka with tomatoes & peppers | 54 |
| Leek & potato soup with crispy bacon & potato chunks | 16 |
| No-bake blueberry cheesecake | 168 |
| Roast lamb & lentil casserole | 70 |
| Sausage & cider casserole | 108 |
| Steak & ale pies | 42 |
| Sticky toffee pud & whiskey caramel sauce | 160 |
| Tomato & basil soup with garlic ciabatta | 14 |

All recipes have been tried, tested and tasted by Sainsbury's, so you can be sure of great results every time

# Index

# Conversion table

| Weights | | Volume | | Measurements | | Oven temperatures | | |
|---|---|---|---|---|---|---|---|---|
| | | | | | | | fan | gas |
| 15g | ½oz | 25ml | 1fl oz | 2mm | 1/16in | 110°C | 90°C | |
| 25g | 1oz | 50ml | 2fl oz | 3mm | ⅛in | 120°C | 100°C | ½ |
| 40g | 1½oz | 75ml | 3fl oz | 4mm | ⅙in | 140°C | 120°C | 1 |
| 50g | 2oz | 100ml | 4fl oz | 5mm | ¼in | 150°C | 130°C | 2 |
| 60g | 2½oz | 150ml | 5fl oz (¼ pint) | 1cm | ½in | 160°C | 140°C | 3 |
| 75g | 3oz | 175ml | 6fl oz | 2cm | ¾in | 180°C | 160°C | 4 |
| 100g | 3½oz | 200ml | 7fl oz | 2.5cm | 1in | 190°C | 170°C | 5 |
| 125g | 4oz | 225ml | 8fl oz | 3cm | 1¼in | 200°C | 180°C | 6 |
| 150g | 5oz | 250ml | 9fl oz | 4cm | 1½in | 220°C | 200°C | 7 |
| 175g | 6oz | 300ml | 10fl oz (½ pint) | 4.5cm | 1¾in | 230°C | 210°C | 8 |
| 200g | 7oz | 350ml | 13fl oz | 5cm | 2in | 240°C | 220°C | 9 |
| 225g | 8oz | 400ml | 14fl oz | 6cm | 2½in | | | |
| 250g | 9oz | 450ml | 16fl oz (¾ pint) | 7.5cm | 3in | | | |
| 275g | 10oz | 600ml | 20fl oz (1 pint) | 9cm | 3½in | | | |
| 300g | 11oz | 750ml | 25fl oz (1¼ pints) | 10cm | 4in | | | |
| 350g | 12oz | 900ml | 30fl oz (1½ pints) | 13cm | 5in | | | |
| 375g | 13oz | 1 litre | 34fl oz (1¾ pints) | 13.5cm | 5¼in | | | |
| 400g | 14oz | 1.2 litres | 40fl oz (2 pints) | 15cm | 6in | | | |
| 425g | 15oz | 1.5 litres | 52fl oz (2½ pints) | 16cm | 6½in | | | |
| 450g | 1lb | 1.8 litres | 60fl oz (3 pints) | 18cm | 7in | | | |
| 500g | 1lb 2oz | | | 19cm | 7½in | | | |
| 650g | 1lb 7oz | | | 20cm | 8in | | | |
| 675g | 1½lb | | | 23cm | 9in | | | |
| 700g | 1lb 9oz | | | 24cm | 9½in | | | |
| 750g | 1lb 11oz | | | 25.5cm | 10in | | | |
| 900g | 2lb | | | 28cm | 11in | | | |
| 1kg | 2lb 4oz | | | 30cm | 12in | | | |
| 1.5kg | 3lb 6oz | | | 32.5cm | 13in | | | |
| | | | | 35cm | 14in | | | |

MIX
Paper from responsible sources
FSC® C023561
www.fsc.org

© Produced by Seven Squared on behalf of Sainsbury's Supermarkets Ltd, 33 Holborn, London EC1N 2HT.
Published August 2010. 
Printed and bound by Butler Tanner and Dennis Ltd, Frome and London.
ISBN-13: 978-0956630308

SEVEN squared